ADDICTED TO INCARCERATION

ADDICTED TO INCARCERATION

Corrections Policy and the Politics of Misinformation in the United States

Travis C. Pratt

Arizona State University

Los Angeles • London • New Delhi • Singapore • Washington DC

For information:

SAGE Publications, Inc.
2455 Teller Road
Thousand Oaks,
California 91320
E-mail: order@sagepub.com

SAGE Publications Ltd.
1 Oliver's Yard
55 City Road
London EC1Y 1SP
United Kingdom

SAGE Publications India Pvt. Ltd.
B 1/I 1 Mohan Cooperative Industrial Area
Mathura Road, New Delhi 110 044
India

SAGE Publications Asia-Pacific Pte. Ltd.
33 Pekin Street #02-01
Far East Square
Singapore 048763

Printed in the United States of America.

Library of Congress Cataloging-in-Publication Data

Pratt, Travis C.
Addicted to incarceration : corrections policy and the politics of misinformation in the United States / Travis C. Pratt.
p. cm.
Includes bibliographical references and index.
ISBN 978-0-7619-2831-7 (cloth)
ISBN 978-0-7619-2832-4 (pbk.)
1. Imprisonment—Government policy—United States.
2. Corrections—Government policy—United States. I. Title.

HV9304.P713 2009
365'.973—dc22 2008019316

This book is printed on acid-free paper.

09 10 11 12 10 9 8 7 6 5 4 3 2

Acquisitions Editor: Jerry Westby
Associate Editor: Lindsay Dutro
Editorial Assistant: Eve Oettinger
Production Editor: Karen Wiley
Copy Editor: Teresa Herlinger
Typesetter: C&M Digitals (P) Ltd.
Proofreader: Andrea Martin
Indexer: Rick Hurd
Cover Designer: Edgar Abarca
Marketing Manager: Christy Guilbault

Contents

Foreword

Personal opinions about crime control policy are influenced by a variety of factors, including misconceptions of justice system processes, overgeneralizations of personal experiences (both direct and vicarious), religious beliefs regarding forgiveness and retribution, sensationalized media accounts of atypical criminal incidents, personal ideologies, and assumptions about human nature. It's not surprising, then, that public discourse on the use of imprisonment to control crime frequently seems clouded, confused, and even contradictory to informed observers. A constructive discussion regarding the utility of imprisonment should begin by minimizing the influence of personal biases and prejudices.

The late John Rawls, who is widely regarded as one of the greatest philosophers of the 20th century, provided a heuristic tool (termed the "veil of ignorance") that can help in this regard. Behind the veil, self-interested actors don't know anything about themselves (e.g., their race, class, sex, and intellectual capabilities). What's more, in this abstracted position individuals must assume that their personal attributes and place in society will ultimately be determined by an enemy. Although Rawls developed this device to identify principles of justice, it can also be used for less ambitious undertakings, such as identifying a few of the basic features of contemporary imprisonment policies. So, for the sake of argument, assume that your adversary assigned you to the following attributes and social location: You are a 22-year-old African American male who resides in a crime-ridden neighborhood located in an economically distressed Rust-Belt city. Your placement comes with a number of social impediments, such as a deadbeat father, an abysmal public education, a lack of legitimate job opportunities, membership in a small social network with depleted reserves of social capital, and a high risk of violent victimization. Put simply, your foe has assigned you to a social position that makes the likelihood that you will be incarcerated during your lifetime very high.

Now, given your impending worldly fate, how would you go about structuring imprisonment practices? Would you employ a tool to predict future offending that is no more reliable than a coin flip to guide selective incapacitation practices? Would you condone the misuse of public opinion data to support punitive sentencing practices? Would you divert taxpayer dollars away from correctional programming to warehouse more prisoners? Of course you wouldn't. Doing so would be against your self-interest and, by definition, completely irrational. Examples of seemingly absurd policies and practices can be identified throughout American government. Criminal justice systems are no exception.

When compared to other Western democracies, the incarceration rate in the United States is staggering. Indeed, if incarcerating citizens was an Olympic sport, the United States would win the Gold Medal. The sheer number of imprisoned Americans and the potential social harm that results necessitate a serious examination of incarceration practices. In *Addicted to Incarceration,* Travis Pratt identifies some widespread misconceptions that have contributed to our current imprisonment policies. Pratt argues that erroneous claims that fear of crime is objectively linked to victimization, that petty offenders mature into violent predators, and that persistent offending can be accurately predicted over the life course constitute a triple-decker justification that many politicians use to promote punitive policies. But the problem, according to Pratt, is not limited to these fallacies. He notes correctly that many policy makers also rely on misleading data from opinion polls to gauge public sentiment about the use of incarceration to control crime. By doing so, politicians claim they're enacting get-tough policies that the public demands. Pratt laments that crudely worded survey questions fail to capture the nuanced nature of public opinion regarding punishment. The misuse of opinion data to champion imprisonment, Pratt charges, has contributed to a slate of official sanctions that doesn't coincide with the wishes of the general public.

Pratt completes his laundry list of misconceptions with a discussion of prisons and crime control. Here, he raises an important point—too much political rhetoric on the impact of imprisonment on crime ignores the fact that multiple factors influence crime rates. This is a source of frustration for a number of criminologists. Social science research from a variety of disciplines and intellectual traditions is clear: we do not live in a bivariate world where all of the variation in variable Y is explained completely by a single factor, variable X. Yet, pundits who promulgate the effectiveness of get-tough sentencing schemes are seldom held accountable for perpetuating such naive and, as Pratt points out, costly arguments. In terms of reducing crime, how costly is imprisonment? Pratt estimates that a 1 percent drop in the crime rate costs American taxpayers between $5.5 and $11 billion in prison expenditures. It's a little ironic that the principal advocates of the incarceration/crime-reduction view are typically political conservatives who purportedly espouse small, efficient forms of government.

In the end, Pratt calls on policy makers to abandon their overreliance on ideology and pseudoscience to shape crime and justice policies. Instead, Pratt advocates the use of rigorous scientific findings to guide governmental crime control efforts, especially the use of imprisonment. The good news for American taxpayers is that a sizable, organized group of researchers (referred to as "criminologists") have dedicated their professional lives to the scientific study of the nature and extent of crime, and how society responds to crime. But, as Pratt points out, criminologists are partly to blame for the current "knowledge gap." This community of scholars has traditionally shied away from making their research findings readily accessible to policy makers and the general public. Some criminologists argue that we know far too little about crime and justice to meaningfully contribute to policy debates. Pratt rejects this position, and challenges criminologists to abandon their overuse of technical jargon, to become more active in promoting their own research, to stop being so equivocal about their research findings, and to develop a more sophisticated understanding of the incentive structures that drive decision making among policy makers. In short, Pratt calls on criminologists to become policy scientists who speak truth to power.

Addicted to Incarceration forces us to closely examine some of the wrong turns we, as a society, have taken in our efforts to combat crime. An open and honest dialogue informed by social scientific findings and devoid of ideological biases and misconceptions about crime and justice is essential if we are to eventually construct a more rational system of justice. Pratt's book represents a positive step in this direction.

Michael D. Reisig
Florida State University

Preface

At the beginning of 2008, the United States had 1 percent of its population behind bars. Our incarcerated population is larger than China's (a nation that dwarfs us in overall population size), and our rate of incarceration is higher than for nations such as South Africa and Iran (nations where one can earn a stint in incarceration for merely holding certain political views; see Pew Charitable Trusts 2008). None of this is an accident. It is instead the result of consistent and purposive policy changes over the last few decades.

Accordingly, the central thesis of this book is that the United States has become "addicted to incarceration." This addiction has been fueled by policies legitimized by faulty information about the crime problem in the United States, American citizens' opinions about crime and punishment, and the efficacy of incarceration as a means of social control. Previous works on incarceration trends have often made the mistake of divorcing punishment policy from the larger social context that generated such policies. This book, on the other hand, takes the wider approach of using trends in incarceration as a common example—or microcosm—of how the politics of punishment (and the politics of misinformation) have influenced criminal justice policy in recent years.

In doing so, the chapters contained in Part I outline the "scope of the problem" with regard to our current practice of incarceration. The introductory chapter highlights the nature of the political discussions surrounding criminal justice policy in general and corrections policy in particular, and explicitly discusses the role of misinformation in how the United States has ended up with its current state of incarceration (i.e., how we got to this state of affairs). The second chapter in this section outlines the processes by which political discourse on crime, criminal justice, and punishment has become more and more politicized since the 1960s. In particular, this discussion addresses how control over the nature of punishment "changed hands" away from correctional professionals and toward political entrepreneurs in the late 1960s in the wake of a general movement to bring the issues of crime and its control to the political forefront.

The three chapters that comprise Part II demonstrate how the policy prescriptions of the last three decades (e.g., mandatory sentences connected to the "war on drugs," three strikes laws) have been based on three different (yet certainly interrelated) forms of misinformation. The first form is misinformation about crime (the topic to be covered in Chapter 3), specifically, the false notion that increases in the "fear of crime" among Americans simply reflect increases in their actual probability of being the victim of a crime—and in particular, a violent crime. This misconception has been central to policy makers' public justifications for the continued growth of incarceration as a response to the fears of their voters. Misinformation about crime also comes in the form of the misconception that low-level offenders (e.g., drug and property offenders) will inevitably graduate to violent offending if they are not immediately locked up. This erroneous assumption has been the linchpin for stiffening the sanctions associated with a host of criminal offenses—not just the violent ones. According to this logic, sentences for even nonserious offenses should be ratcheted up if one assumes that today's jaywalker is tomorrow's murderer. On a related note, misinformation about crime has also produced the false assumption that chronic, life-course persistent offending can be accurately predicted using variables that are given the most "weight" in criminal justice processing: the severity of the offender's present offense and his or her prior record.

The second source of misinformation to be examined in Part II has to do with policy makers' concerns over the desires and attitudes of the American public (the topic of Chapter 4). While political advocates of mass incarceration consistently contend that they are merely being responsive to the demands of their constituents (i.e., they are simply giving the public what it wants), the research presented in Chapter 4 demonstrates that Americans' views on crime and punishment are far more complex than policy makers generally care to admit. While Americans do harbor fairly punitive "global" opinions about crime and the use of incarceration, a number of studies have demonstrated that, when it gets to the "specifics," Americans also support the philosophy and practice of correctional rehabilitation (even if they still place considerable faith in deterrence and incapacitation approaches). Americans are also quite supportive of early intervention strategies with juveniles and alternatives to incarceration (especially for nonserious drug offenders). The broad point of Chapter 4 is that policy makers have outpaced the desires of the American public to increase the punitiveness of punishment policies.

The third source of misinformation in Part II concerns the efficacy of incarceration as a crime control strategy (the topic covered in Chapter 5). The specific focus of this chapter is the empirical status of the research that scholars have produced in an effort to uncover whether prison expansion and related policy efforts actually reduce crime. In all, the evidence in favor of "prisons for crime control" is fairly scarce. The reasons behind such weak "incapacitation effects" are also explored in this chapter—in particular, the comparative validity of the "bad implementation" (e.g., "we're just not tough enough") versus the "incomplete theory of offender decision making" explanations for why locking up more and more offenders does not seem to do much to the crime rate. The general conclusion reached in Chapter 5 is that prisons, at best, provide little in the way of a crime control return for our public dollar.

The chapters in Part III go on to discuss the various social costs of incarceration. These costs come in the form of how incarceration has replaced other social institutions (e.g., public and mental health care) that were previously charged with the tasks of dealing with public problems; how incarceration (especially the way incarceration is done in the United States) has heightened the risk of personal victimization for inmates and has become a barrier to successful offender reintegration into society; how recent trends in the spatial distribution of the communities from which our primary incarcerated population is drawn have contributed to the further breakdown of inner-city environments; how incarceration has reinforced and exacerbated existing racial inequalities; and how our need to provide additional prison space has resulted in the state's abdication of punishment to the private sphere and what the profit motive has done (and is continuing to do) to the practice of punishment.

The book ends with the suggestion of a number of strategies to combat our dependence on incarceration. These include emphasizing the practice and philosophy of correctional rehabilitation, developing early intervention strategies with juvenile offenders, and reinvesting in community corrections. The point here is not to be preachy, but rather to offer up "evidence-based" crime control policy alternatives to incarceration. By shining a spotlight on the misinformation surrounding our current punishment practices, perhaps the work presented here may, at minimum, serve as a catalyst for a more informed public discussion about our reliance on prisons as the primary mechanism for social control.

Travis C. Pratt
Arizona State University

Acknowledgments

When it comes to books, brevity can be deceptive. Despite its short length, this book took a frighteningly long time to complete. I take full responsibility for the glacial pace for which it finally came together, even in the face of the best efforts of many of those around me to keep me on track. Their support and input were both tireless and patient, regardless of how committed I seemed to letting the project linger on indefinitely. Accordingly, like any "individual" accomplishment, a number of people were critical to the ideas, writing, and content contained in this book, but as much as I'd like to lay the blame for any errors or omissions on their shoulders, they're all mine.

Many thanks are due to Les Kennedy, for opening the door for this project in the first place; Jerry Westby, for his continued patience with me at every stage of the book's development; and all of the reviewers of earlier drafts of the book for their helpful comments and suggestions:

Gaylene Armstrong, Sam Houston State University

Andrew Austin, University of Wisconsin Green Bay

Mary Bosworth, Oxford University

Craig Hemmens, Boise State University

James Jengeleski, Shippensburg University

Rick Jones, Marquette University

Dennis Loo, Cal Poly Pomona

Faith Lutze, Washington State University

L. L. Miller, Penn State University

William Perrill, University of Northern Colorado

J. Keith Price, West Texas A&M

Tanya Settles, University of Texas at San Antonio

A special thanks to Natasha Frost, Northeastern University, and Stephen Owen, Radford University, who were particularly helpful; the many undergraduate students at Washington State University who were subjected to early drafts of certain chapters and were unfailing in their willingness to point out any and all problems or inconsistencies in the text; to Teresa Herlinger for her careful editing and suggestions, and to Mike Reisig, both for writing the foreword to the book and for his continued concern that I not embarrass myself with my published work (that I still often do is my fault, not his).

Finally, I'd like to thank my wife, Jodie—a great copy editor, source of ideas, and support who knows more about publishing than many practicing criminologists. Thank you, as always, for sticking with me.

PART I

In December of 2007, a 10-year-old girl was arrested at her elementary school in Florida for possession of a deadly weapon—a knife. She was subsequently charged with possession of a weapon on school property. In addition to the prospect of facing felony charges, she was also suspended from school for 10 days. Yet school officials conceded that she neither brandished said weapon nor threatened anyone with it. Instead, she was using it to cut the steak she had brought from home for lunch (something she had done multiple times in the past).

Because of the school district's "zero tolerance" stance on school violence—a position wholly consistent with the "get tough on crime" movement that the United States has been entrenched in for the last few decades—the girl was transported to and held in the Juvenile Assessment Center in Marion County. Apparently, the unquestioned faith of our citizenry in the efficacy and necessity of getting tough—including teachers (who reported the incident), whose job it is, theoretically, to *think*—we are even incarcerating (albeit for a brief time) 10-year-old girls who are polite enough to not eat steak with their fingers.

How did we get to the point where incarceration is viewed as a desirable response to the proper use of kitchen cutlery by a 5th grader (assuming that the creation of such zero-tolerance policies was not the result of random happenstance)? How did we abandon the philosophy of optimism concerning the individualized treatment of the offender—one that served corrections for well over a century—in favor of one that assumes a stint in a secure correctional facility is the best way to deal with the crime problem? What are the arguments that political leaders have made in an effort to convince citizens that continuing to expand prisons the way we have over the last three decades provides a net social benefit to society?

This section addresses this progression of events. Put simply, the "get tough" movement in crime control policy was no accident. It grew out of a series of changes in the social context that resulted in a change in thinking concerning crime and punishment. No longer would policy makers view these issues as public problems that are impossible to solve. Instead, they would see them as opportunities to gain political capital.

Our addiction to incarceration is the result of that shift. The metaphor of addiction contained in this book is also no accident—the political reliance on the use and expansion of incarceration bears an eerie resemblance to the habits and lifestyles of chronic substance abusers (e.g., exaggerated benefits, denial of evidence of harm, attitudes and rationalizations that excuse use and abuse). This section explores the creation of the incarceration addiction among correctional policy makers.

One

Introduction

When it comes to crime and punishment, the United States has maintained a curious paradox over the last few decades. On the one hand, we have constructed the biggest prison system on the planet. Although we were once relegated to second place in the incarceration race, Russia's release of more than 100,000 inmates in the year 2000—largely over concerns about high levels of crowding and the spread of disease among the inmate population (Mauer 1999)—has allowed the United States to recapture the world's imprisonment crown. Driven primarily by policies emerging out of a conservative contemporary political culture (see Young and Brown 1993) that places enormous faith in the ability to control crime through incarceration, the inmate population in the United States has now topped the 2 million mark.

Given this figure, it is important to note that the exponential growth in the prison population over the last few decades has occurred in the midst of a relatively *stable* violent crime rate over the same period of time (LaFree and Drass 2002). For example, Figure 1.1 shows the increase in incarceration since 1980—a clear linear trend upward. At the same time, Figure 1.2 clearly shows a general pattern of stable (and for some offenses, declining) violent crime rates dating back to 1973.

On the other hand, the United States has also been, and continues to be, the most violent industrialized nation in the world. For example, although the United States incarceration rate is over six times that of England and Australia, for every 100 homicides occurring in Los Angeles there are 4.8 in Sydney and 3.8 in London (Zimring and Hawkins 1997). Furthermore, as can be seen in Table 1.1, the homicide rate in the United States is more than five times that of Canada and more than six times that of nearly every Western European nation (Pratt and Godsey 2003). Even within the United States, Currie (1998) noted that the homicide rate for young African American males more than doubled from 1985 to 1993, to 167 per 100,000 citizens (by way of comparison, it was 46 in 1960). Among the industrialized countries in the world, lethal violence appears to be a uniquely American problem.

The Politics and Consequences of Incarceration

It is apparent, therefore, that our willingness to lock up such a large proportion of the American citizenry has failed to result in a corresponding increase in public safety. Oddly enough, however, this nugget of reality continues to be ignored by public policy makers, many of whom still cling to the misguided notion that we can "build our way out of the crime problem." There are certainly a few variations on the theme, but the overall message from political pundits has been disturbingly homogeneous since the early 1970s: the "crime problem" (such as it is) in this country is the result of chronic leniency on the part of the criminal justice system.

Figure 1.1 U.S. Incarceration Rate, 1980–2006

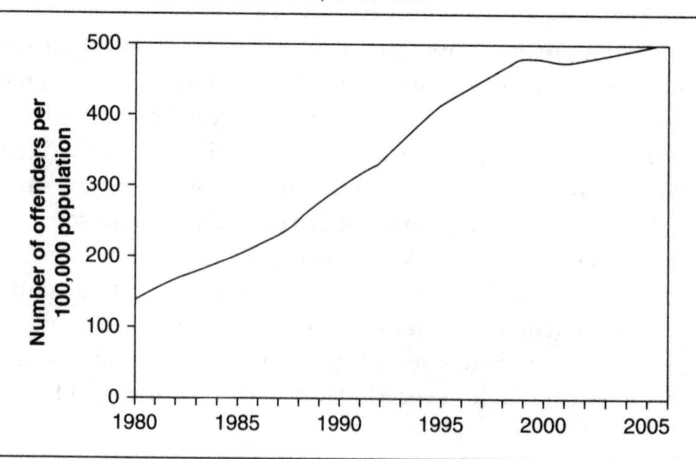

Source: Bureau of Justice Statistics, 2006a.

Figure 1.2 U.S. Rates of Violent Crime, 1973–2003

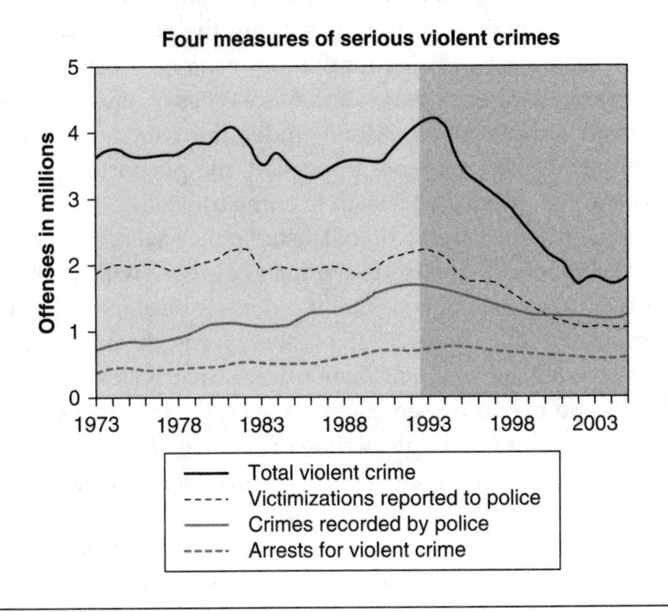

Source: Bureau of Justice Statistics, 2008.

Table 1.1 Comparison of U.S. Homicide Rate (Homicides per 100,000 Citizens) With Other Western Industrialized Nations

Nation	*Homicide Rate*
United States	9.45
United Kingdom	0.90
France	1.10
The Netherlands	1.10
Germany	1.20
Australia	3.35
Canada	1.85

Source: Pratt & Godsey, 2003.

Accordingly, those who oppose this claim are generally treated as having inadvertently confessed to being an intellectual hack (or perhaps to possessing a childlike faith in a more naive-utopian social support approach). Despite the bulk of the research generated by criminologists—who are often pigeonholed by political elites as merely being left-leaning naysayers—policy makers from both sides of the political spectrum have consistently embraced policies that stiffen sentences for more types of offenses (especially drug offenses) and more types of offenders (especially nonviolent and youthful offenders) under the rubric of concern over public safety and, perhaps more important, the purported general effectiveness of the "get tough" approach to crime control.

What makes the get-tough criminal justice policy agenda so seductive for political stakeholders (defined as individuals or groups with a vested interest in a particular policy outcome) is that it can never be empirically (i.e., scientifically) falsified (Cullen et al. 2002). In other words, the most methodologically rigorous available research demonstrates that policies such as "three strikes" laws and enhanced sentences, bloating the prison population even further, and sticking a higher proportion of juvenile offenders in adult facilities have little to no appreciable impact on crime rates (see Fass and Pi 2002; Pratt and Cullen 2005; Visher 1987). Nevertheless, advocates of the get-tough approach may still contend that we just aren't being tough enough (Bennett, DiIulio, and Walters 1996), and that we simply need to "get tougher." As an echo of this sentiment, the calls for alternative approaches to crime control have diminished in recent years (e.g., community supervision or correctional rehabilitation, emphasizing the importance of prisoner reentry programs), and the prison boom has gone on unabated (Pratt, Maahs, and Stehr 1998)—the end result of which forms the central thesis of this book: that the United States has become "addicted to incarceration."

Race, Gender, and Incarceration

Aside from its failure to keep American citizens any safer, our reliance on the use of incarceration as the primary tool for social control has had enormous social costs in recent years. One of the most visible consequences has been the effect of imprisonment trends on the African American community. The incarceration rate for African Americans is currently seven times that of whites (Bureau of Justice Statistics 2006a). Even more telling is the fact that 1 out of every 3 African American men in the United States population between the ages of 20 and 29 is under some form of correctional supervision (prison, jail, probation, or parole); when limited to urban areas, that figure approaches 1 in 2. Although national statistics indicate that the proportion of violent crimes committed by African Americans is higher than it is for whites (Blumstein 2000; Fox 2000), that proportion has stayed fairly constant over the years despite the extreme growth of the African American inmate population. It is therefore safe to conclude that criminal justice policy changes since the early 1980s—most notably the constellation of policies emanating out of the so-called war on drugs and our resulting willingness to incarcerate nonviolent, drug-only offenders—are the most likely culprits for the current racial disparity in our nation's prisons (see also J. Miller 1996).

These policy changes have also significantly impacted the gender gap in imprisonment. The United States Bureau of Justice Statistics indicates that in 1970 there were just over 5,600 women in state and federal prisons. By 2006, that number had increased to over 112,000 (a jump of over 2,000 percent). Upon adding in the nearly 64,000 women currently being held in jail facilities, we find that there are over 175,000 incarcerated women in this country on any given day (Bureau of Justice Statistics 2006a). As with their male counterparts, this increase is even more striking when the numbers are disaggregated by race, where the incarceration rate for African American women today is actually higher than it was for white *men* as recently as 1980. Since women are more likely to be incarcerated for nonviolent and minor offenses than men (especially drug and property offenses)—and typically have fewer prior convictions than men—our preference for imprisoning such offenders anyway has made African American women the fastest growing segment of the United States population under state supervision, where their annual growth rate of admission to prison is roughly twice that of men (Bureau of Justice Statistics 2006a; see also Mauer and Huling 1995).

The Economic Impact of Incarceration

Aside from the negligible impact on crime rates and the disproportionate impact on inner-city minority communities, where has the American addiction to incarceration gotten us? First of all, incarceration has become an integral part of the United States economy. Nowhere is this truer than in rural America, where the construction of new prisons holds the promise of stable jobs and a general boost to stumbling local economies. California's Pelican Bay "supermax" facility (the sexy moniker designating a super-maximum security prison), for instance, was built in the state's poorest county, where the unemployment rate hovered around 26 percent. With the addition of the facility, unemployment dropped to around 10 percent in 1999—still fairly high by national standards, but considerably better than it was before (Tamaki 2000).

Similar results have been found elsewhere as well. One of the most colorful examples is how the tiny town of Tamms, Illinois—with an unemployment rate of 16 percent, a poverty rate above 30 percent, and where half of the households squeak by on less than $15,000 a year—has embraced its supermax prison. In an interesting intersection of punishment, commerce, and pop culture, a local bank in Tamms features a billboard promising "super-max-imum savings," and a local burger joint—the Burger Shack 2—now offers the "Supermax Burger" that, according to Hallinan (2001), apparently comes with "the works."

The American penchant for punishment has also transformed the role of the state over the last three decades. We now live in a nation where the prison industry currently does $50 billion a year in business, and correctional expenditures in general are up over $60 billion (see Figure 1.3). In the state of California, 1 out of every 6 state employees works for the department of corrections. As prison expenditures have assumed a larger proportion of state budgets, a few states (most notably, California and New York) are currently spending more on incarceration than they are on higher education (Bureau of Justice Statistics, 2007a). This shift in spending priorities away from supportive public institutions and toward a more punitive "coercive state" is even more obvious when placed in an international perspective. For example, the World Health Organization's 2000 report indicates that Sweden and Switzerland devote over 10 percent more of their annual gross domestic product (GDP) to health care than the United States does—for Germany, that figure is nearly 30 percent more. Furthermore, both New Zealand and Finland earmark nearly 40 percent more of their annual GDP for education than the United States does, and both Sweden and Denmark spend over 50 percent more of their GDP on education.

Political Justifications for Incarceration

Why has this mixed set of priorities been allowed to continue? One commonly touted explanation is that our political leaders are simply too weak to stand up to the prison industry's special interests and instead routinely cave in to their requests for additional funding and increased protection from the whims of the market (see the discussion in Cressey 1978). Although there may be a kernel of truth to this sentiment, it is highly oversimplified. At best, political discussions about the condition of the criminal justice system in the United States have merely been uncritical, as political

Figure 1.3 U.S. Criminal Justice Expenditures, 1982–2005

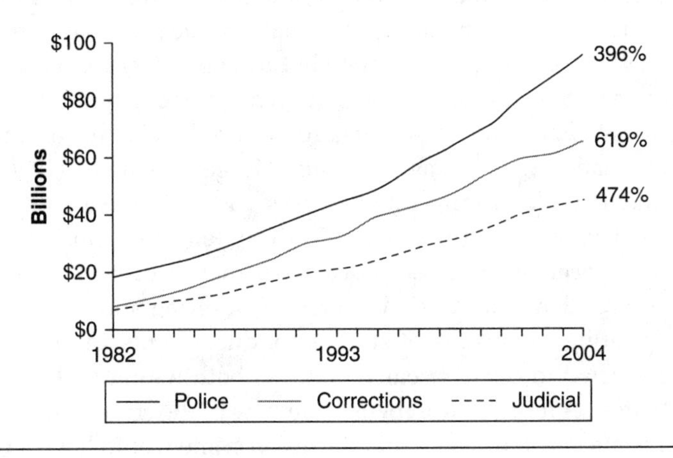

Source: Bureau of Justice Statistics, 2007a.

candidates routinely ignore the sticky issue of mass incarceration in favor of focusing on the more symbolic notions of "victims' rights" and "personal responsibility" (see Gilsinan 1991; J. Q. Wilson 1997).

Going a step further, Currie (1998, 6) has argued that a more significant contributor to the "knowledge gap" between public policy makers and American citizens is that

> people are genuinely confused about what to think about the state of crime and punishment in America. And they are confused in part because they are continually bombarded with the myths, misconceptions, and half-truths that dominate public discussion.

While Currie's comments are important (and certainly accurate) in their own right, they miss a key element of the political trend in contemporary punishment, and one that is a core focus of this book. In particular, since the early 1970s political decision makers have found that a considerable amount of political capital can be gained by calling attention to the "crime problem," by framing this problem as the inevitable outcome of the 1960s culture of social permissiveness and a criminal justice system dominated by rehabilitation-minded liberal Pollyannas, and by generating as much public support as possible for repressive crime control policies (Beckett 1997; see also Gest 2001).

In the end, misinformation about crime and punishment is touted as the Truth, as new generations of policy makers ride piggyback on the "get tough" rhetoric of their predecessors. In turn, policy makers can continue their ongoing public pillow fights about who can be tougher than whom. In the process, bad information gets reproduced. Take, for example, the comments made by the Texas economist Morgan Reynolds (1996, 3) that "Punishment works. Incarceration works." Reynolds was only able to make this claim by citing research selectively (e.g., by ignoring the body of published, peer-reviewed empirical work that points to a different conclusion; see Cullen et al. 2002; Visher 1987; Zimring and Hawkins 1995) and by ignoring the results of studies conducted outside of Texas (e.g., those conducted in other research contexts both within and outside the United States). A more comprehensive review of the criminological literature on the effects of punishment policies on crime would have led him to a much different conclusion (see, e.g., Pratt and Cullen 2005).

Furthermore, information about the extent of our reliance on incarceration will sometimes get perverted so that political stakeholders can make it "look good" for their own purposes. As a case in point, when Bill Clinton was running for his second term as president, one of the members of his administration boldly noted—presumably in an effort to show how great the last 4 years had been—that "more people are at work, more people are off the welfare roles, and *more people are in prison*" (see Currie 1999, 9, emphasis added). While greater numbers of employed citizens and reduced welfare roles both typically garner public support from both ends of the political spectrum, the logic of the last point is quite troubling. As Currie (1999) has noted, it would be difficult to believe that the American Medical Association would interpret a rise in the number of hospitalized cancer patients as evidence that we are "winning the war" against the disease.

Just as important as the perpetuation of bad information and the political distortion of better information, accurate information about crime and punishment is rarely reviewed by policy makers since such material is typically found in outlets that policy makers rarely read—the dreaded academic journals. The studies published in these journals are the most scientifically rigorous available, yet the "reality" of crime and punishment contained in this body of work is more difficult to "sell," largely because of the way academics present it. These studies are often quite complex quantitatively and therefore not terribly accessible to those not privy to the secret academic handshake. Alternatively, the standard "get tough" rhetoric of political pundits is more easily adoptable—and more easily absorbed by citizens—because of the simple bumper-sticker eloquence of the message. As but merely one example of the political allure of syllabically efficient criminological explanations, who could forget Bob Dole's statement during the 1996 U.S. presidential campaign: "I know what causes crime: Criminals. Criminals. Criminals."

Two

The Politics of Punishment in the United States

It was not that long ago that our nation's incarceration rate was relatively stable, with no real indication that it would be escalating anytime soon (Blumstein and Cohen 1973). Among criminologists, there was even talk of "decarceration"—uttered with a straight face, no less—in conjunction with a more general perception that current forms of punishment should be viewed as a "vestigial carryover of a barbaric past" that would "disappear as humanitarianism and rationality spread" (Toby 1964, 332; see also J. Miller 1991; Mitford 1971; Scull 1977). During this time period, it seemed that the practice of punishment was headed on a relatively progressive trajectory, where capital punishment was abolished in the United States as a result of the Supreme Court's *Furman v. Georgia* (1972) decision, the federal judiciary intervened in the daily operations of prison management to address what the courts viewed as unacceptably harsh institutional conditions (DiIulio 1987), and even certain nonlethal forms of punishment—such as Delaware's whipping post (bearing the name "Red Hannah"), which was used as a punishment for misbehaving inmates—fell by the wayside (Newman 1985).

My, how times have changed. With the benefit of hindsight we can see that these early predictions regarding the direction punishment policy would take were so far off the mark that such pundits would soon be scratching their heads in genuine puzzlement over how they could have been so wrong. In just a short period, we have gone from a time in which punishment and incarceration were seen as politically passé to "a time in which punishment dominates policy discussions and the prison is embraced as the linchpin of the nation's response to crime" (Cullen, Fisher, and Applegate 2000, 2). Given this state of affairs, we might ask ourselves a couple of logical questions: What caused this shift in how we think about crime and punishment? How did this transformation seemingly catch criminologists off guard? In an effort to address these questions, this chapter traces the sequence of events that resulted in the political control over punishment policy in general—and corrections policy in particular—that is most responsible for our current state of mass incarceration.

In doing so, a brief historical overview of the broad changes in corrections policy over the last century is necessary. Since comprehensive historical accounts of American punishment practices can be found elsewhere (see, e.g., L. M. Friedman 1993; Garland 1990), an attempt at such a sweeping analysis will not be made here. Instead, this discussion will be focused on two central issues: the general shifts in the ways Americans have viewed the "causes" of crime since the early 1900s, and how these shifts have influenced what kinds of "solutions" to the crime problem end up working their way into correctional policy and practice.

The theme running throughout this chapter—which is typically absent from academic discussions of corrections policy—is the extent to which policy prescriptions are determined by how the "problem" (in this case, the crime problem) is defined. For example, historical changes in punishment practices have been motivated by at least three factors associated with changes in the social and political context: (1) the feelings of hostility and desires for revenge that criminal offenders arouse in their victims and those who sympathize with the victims; (2) abstract normative philosophies, ideologies, and religious beliefs regarding punishment; and (3) prevailing theories of crime causation (Pratt et al. 1998; see also Newman 1985). Although these motives and rationales can and often do operate simultaneously, the relative power afforded to each depends on which policy stakeholders are able to control how the crime problem should be defined at any given point in time—a concept that has been referred to among corrections scholars as "problem ownership" (Pratt et al. 1998).

In a more general sense, Gusfield (1981, 10) states that the ownership of problems

> is derived from the recognition that in the arenas of public opinion and debate all groups do not have equal power, influence, and authority to define the reality of the problem. . . . The metaphor of property ownership is chosen to emphasize the attributes of control, exclusiveness, transferability, and potential loss also found in the ownership of property.

In short, whoever can present the most persuasive version of the *cause* of the problem under investigation is then in the best position to market their proposed *solution* to that problem. Thus, problem ownership refers to how a particular group of policy stakeholders may come to define the ideological boundaries of an issue (in the present case, to dominate discussions of the purported cause of crime) and are given the authority to set the political agenda associated with that policy area—in this case, to provide the most politically persuasive solution to the crime problem (Kingdon 1995).

The remainder of this chapter discusses the development of corrections policy in the context of which groups of policy stakeholders were able to exert control over American punishment practices at various points in time. After tracing certain historical trends, the discussion then turns to how "law and order" political rhetoric and expansions in the use of incarceration since the early 1970s have become intertwined—so much so that the two appear to be joined at the hip in a kind of sick and twisted codependent dance. The end result, of course, is the unfortunate, yet seemingly unquestioned, faith among our political leaders in the social utility of mass incarceration.

Problem Ownership, Punishment Philosophies, and Changes in Corrections Policy Over Time

Pre-Progressive Era Corrections Policy

A firm understanding of how we have arrived at our current state of incarceration requires a grasp of linear trends in punishment philosophies and corrections policies over time. To reach this understanding, this discussion begins in the early 20th century, when the size and scope of public programs (i.e., the state) in the United States were rather small, and when the rise of "modern corrections" took place (Rothman 1980).

In the wake of a changing social and economic climate, and coupled with the political demands of a growing middle class, the state began to play a larger role in society (Staples 1990). As a result, this period was characterized by increasing governmental activity in the areas of transportation, banking, and many other commercial enterprises, as well as the arena of social control that resulted in the "business" of punishment and corrections being co-opted by the state (Pratt et al. 1998). During this time (roughly the late 1800s to the early 1900s), the problems of crime and incarceration focused primarily on the morality of the offender. This emphasis was largely a holdover from the earliest American attempts at institutional corrections in general (which were borrowed in no small part from prison reformer John Howard's efforts in England). Most notably, the Pennsylvania and New York (Auburn) systems (those that were most influential in that part of the 19th century) stressed the importance of religion for resisting the moral temptations that criminal behavior may provide (Clear, Cole, and Reisig 2006).

Not surprisingly, the theory of criminal behavior that was central to the practice of corrections at this time was the classical school of criminology's simple emphasis on rational choice. Stated clearly, the rational choice perspective viewed criminal activity as the consequence of how an individual's moral code (or lack thereof) affects the way he or she evaluates the potential costs and benefits of criminal activity (Cullen and Gilbert 1982); that is, one's cost–benefit calculation is guided by one's moral compass. Accordingly, since the advent of what can be termed "modern" institutional corrections up to the early 1900s, the American sociopolitical context was ripe for corrections policy being heavily infused with a particular brand of religion. The architects of corrections policy at this time, who were operating with both feet planted firmly within the Judeo-Christian ethic, assumed that a liberal helping of religious indoctrination, via incarceration, would induce the necessary "penitence" (hence, the term "penitentiary") to lead the offender back to the path of a moral life (Clear 1994; Foucalt 1977).

Moreover, the states' efforts to realign the cost–benefit calculus of the offenders who were under their control did not stop merely at passive Christian inculcation—most states added hard labor and a host of public punishments (e.g., stocks with hunched inmates' heads and hands sticking through a wooden sandwich) to incarceration (Hirsch 1992). Nevertheless, the overriding purpose of the prison system at this time was to isolate offenders from the morally corrupted influences in which their lives had become entrenched (and, in some cases, to isolate them from each other), so that "while engaged in productive labor, they could reflect on their past misdeeds, repent, and be reformed" (Clear et al. 2006, 42; see also McKelvey 1977; Newman 1985).

Even more indicative of the spiritual emphasis in corrections policy during this historical period is the way female prison inmates were treated. While still rooted in the working assumption of the morality–crime nexus, female offenders were viewed as the victims of immoral men (Feinman 1986). Therefore, prison facilities for female offenders were to be staffed and managed by females only. Such an arrangement was due to an intense belief at this time that coeducational facilities—where female inmates would be comingling with either male inmates or male staff—would simply reinforce the same gender-based lapses in morality that brought women to such facilities in the first place (Freedman 1974). Thus, female inmates were to receive large doses of religious treatment—often cloaked under the guise of programs teaching traditional wife/mother values and domestic skills (e.g., food preparation, sewing, and what we now call cosmetology)—in an effort to set them back on the path of righteousness (Dobash, Dobash, and Gutteridge 1986; Morash, Haarr, and Rucker 1994).

The increasing momentum of the Progressive movement, however, which began in the late 1800s and reached its zenith in the early 1920s, resulted in a fundamental realignment of the state–society relationship. The shifting social and political context of the early 20th century fueled a change in the American consensus regarding what the primary purpose of incarceration should be. In particular, the Progressive Era ushered in a new conception of the role of the state and saw the rise of scientific positivism,[1] which provided an empirical foundation—and therefore an ideological justification—for a change in punishment philosophy and correctional practice.

Positive Science and Agency Autonomy in the Progressive Era

Owing to the expansion of the public sector in the early 20th century, the faith-based dominance in corrections policy lost momentum as the public services began to explicitly adopt the principles of science as a tool for addressing public problems (Staples 1990). The notion that science could play a significant part in shaping effective public policy gained credence throughout the Progressive Era, when upper- and middle-class Progressives began to place considerable faith in the ability of the state to effectively handle such complex issues as immigration, labor and working conditions, and rapid urbanization (Knott and Miller 1987). The acceptance of science as a legitimate tool for structuring the delivery of public services also led to a shift in control over corrections policy away from religious pundits and toward the scientific professionals (and their respective agencies) who were charged with the task of managing and transforming the behavior of inmates. It was the influence of such professionals, along with their belief in a new scientific view of human behavior, that fueled the social acceptance of a new approach for understanding the apparent causes of—and therefore solutions to—crime.

Admittedly, many of the early positivist perspectives on crime causation that were adopted by progressive-minded correctional reformers can (and should) be viewed as existing somewhere between being overly simple and downright laughable. To be sure, early criminologists attributed criminal behavior to certain physical characteristics (most notably, the shape of the skull; Lombroso-Ferrero 1911), to a lack of intelligence (often referred to as "feeblemindedness"; Goddard 1914), or to some unfortunate—as yet predetermined—destiny where genetically inferior parents would pass on to their offspring the genetic code that would make crime/deviance almost inevitable (see the review in McGloin and Pratt 2003). As a result, terms such as "ativists" (born criminals who were throwbacks to a more primitive species) and "fidgety Phils" (what we may now refer to as youths with ADHD; see Pratt et al. 2002) entered the criminological (and correctional) lexicon.

At this same time, however, criminologists were beginning to catalogue certain social factors, such as poor access to quality education and conditions of economic deprivation, which may also explain situational offending. By the late 1920s, psychology and sociology began to provide the dominant (in other words, more socially persuasive) explanations for crime. For example, psychological explanations became more sophisticated with the introduction of Freud's personality-based developmental theory in the early 20th century, and Shaw and McKay's (1942) social disorganization perspective focused on the societal conditions that produced high-crime areas within cities. Shaw and McKay's work, in turn, provided the basis for strain theory, social control theory, and differential association theory—three of the most popular contemporary sociological frameworks for understanding crime (Lilly, Cullen, and Ball 2007). Despite their conceptual differences, these new sociological and psychological theories of crime causation shared a central thesis: human behavior is not determined at birth and, with proper treatment, inappropriate behaviors (such as criminal and delinquent behavior) can be modified.

But not just any old treatment would do. The key for correctional Progressives was individualized treatment according to the needs of the individual offender (Rothman 1980). In sharp contrast to the approach taken by correctional reformers of the 19th century, this new movement in punishment rejected the notion of a one-size-fits-all protocol (religion and labor) for effecting behavioral change in offenders. Instead, Progressives highlighted the importance of gaining intimate knowledge of the unique problems facing each offender and then devising a treatment plan that would be tailored to that individual. Consequently, correctional staff would need to be the principal players in the process of diagnosing the factors to be targeted for change for each offender, prescribing and carrying out the specified treatment plan, and determining the timing of release (Rothman 1980).

As a result, administrative professionals within prisons—including those assumed to be trained experts at behavior modification—were able to exert more control over correctional policy and practice and were given wide discretionary authority to administer therapeutic strategies for treating inmates (Pratt et al. 1998). As crime became viewed as a symptom of a quasi-medical condition or social breakdown, corrections agency professionals' authority over punishment practices was translated into punishment policy with the advent of more formalized community sanctions (probation and parole release) and, most important, the indeterminate sentencing system.

Under indeterminate sentencing schemes, state and federal statutes allowed judges to sentence offenders to a wide range of time under state control. For example, felony sentences ranging from 1 to 20 years for any given offense would not have been uncommon (Goodstein and Hepburn 1985). The reason for doing so was consistent with the model of individual treatment: as soon as the offender had been successfully rehabilitated, he or she would be released into the community. The assumption was that, since individuals differ according to what caused them to engage in criminal behavior, and since not all individuals respond in identical ways to various treatment protocols, there is a need for a flexible sentencing system that allows correctional treatment providers to tailor their interventions to the individual needs of offenders (Cullen and Gilbert 1982).

In most states in the early 20th century, indeterminate sentences were coupled with the practice of parole release. By the 1920s, over 80 percent of all offenders sentenced to prison were released via the mechanism of parole (Clear et al. 2006). In yet another way that corrections agency professionals solidified their control over correctional policy during this time, parole release—a decision left to correctional administrators—was even used as a method for undermining political efforts to increase the maximum penalties for certain offenses (i.e., the upper end of the indeterminate sentence). This "back end" release mechanism thus provided parole decision makers with even wider discretionary authority.

The philosophy of rehabilitation (brought about through the individualized treatment of offenders) was intimately intertwined with corrections policy up until the late 1960s. During this time, skepticism among policy makers and the general public began to emerge regarding the malleability of offenders and the legitimacy of the practice of correctional treatment. This erosion of confidence began to weaken corrections agency professionals' control over corrections policy just as the crime problem started to emerge as a salient issue in American politics.

From Experts to Politicians: Contemporary Trends in Corrections Policy

The United States experienced a dramatic rise in crime rates in the late 1960s. Levels of criminal victimization for a host of offenses (primarily violent crimes) reached an all-time high, and public concern over this trend grew just as quickly (Beckett 1997; Rothman 1980). Something had to be responsible for the crime wave, and fingers started pointing at our correctional system. As a result, the rehabilitative ideal came under considerable ideological and empirical attack, leaving corrections policy in a state of "crisis" (Cullen and Gilbert 1982, 1).

Fueling this crisis were three interrelated developments. First, a review of 231 studies regarding the effectiveness of various correctional treatment and rehabilitation strategies conducted between 1945 and 1967 was released by Robert Martinson (1974). His assessment of the evidence led him to conclude in a now famous (or perhaps infamous) statement that "with few and isolated exceptions, the rehabilitative efforts that have been reported so far have had no appreciable effect on recidivism" (p. 25). Others had reached this conclusion before (Conrad 1973; Doleschal and Klamputs 1973), yet none had the public impact of Martinson's work (see the discussion in Pratt 2002). Alternatively, Martinson's (1979) considerably less famous recant of his earlier conclusion, along with the more rehabilitation-friendly full monograph by Lipton, Martinson, and Wilks (1975), was not so warmly embraced by correctional policy makers. Instead, Martinson's original (1974) work was taken as proof of what policy makers (and the American public) were already beginning to believe:

that "rehabilitation doesn't work." It was the perceived failure of rehabilitation that provided the foundation for a political assault on the autonomy of corrections agency professionals.

Second, the social conservative movement of the 1970s contributed to the crisis in corrections policy as both citizens and policy makers began to question the utility and fairness of the sentencing flexibility afforded to judges (as well as the "back end" release mechanism of parole) that had been the staple of the rehabilitative ideal for the greater part of the previous half-century. In essence, conservatives held that the indeterminate sentencing framework, where a wide range of sentence lengths could conceivably be given to various offenders who had committed the same offense, tended to result in sentences that fell well short of the maximum penalty prescribed by law. This sentiment was echoed by the common practice of early release via parole (Latessa and Allen 2003). As such, conservative policy makers argued that the practice and philosophy of correctional rehabilitation, with its reliance on sentencing flexibility, amounted to little more than "coddling" offenders (Cullen and Gilbert 1982).

The solution, then, for those aligned with the conservative movement was threefold: (1) abolish indeterminate sentences, (2) eliminate parole release, and (3) institute a system of determinate—or fixed/flat—sentences. And states did just that; sentencing grids became commonplace, where offenders would be sentenced according to a narrow range of options based on their current offenses and prior criminal record. In addition, a number of prison release mechanisms (most of which were attached in some way to parole) were curtailed considerably (Goodstein and Hepburn 1985). The end result of these policy changes was that corrections agency professionals turned over their discretion to call the shots with regard to the ultimate penalty phase of the criminal justice process to lawmakers.

Third, at the same time that the conservative camp was advocating the abolition of the indeterminate sentence (and, with it, the rehabilitative ideal), the liberal community in the United States became divided on the issue. While one (albeit small) portion of the liberal minded still championed correctional rehabilitation and therefore stressed the necessity of the indeterminate sentence for effective correctional treatment (see, e.g., Palmer 1974, 1975; see also Palmer and Lewis 1980), a second group emerged: the "justice model liberals" (Pratt et al. 1998).

This group also advocated the abandonment of the rehabilitative ideal and the indeterminate sentence, yet for a much different reason from that of the conservatives. Rather than seeing indeterminate sentences as being too soft on offenders, justice model liberals sought to reduce the discretionary authority of prison officials because they viewed them as agents of unfair coercive practices (Cullen and Gendreau 1989). Much of this concern had to do with the findings of judicial and scholarly inquiries into correctional operations during the 1970s. This work uncovered widespread instances of prisoner abuse and manipulation (Feeley and Rubin 1998; see also *Brooks v. Florida* 1967; *Holt v. Sarver* 1971), deteriorating conditions of incarceration that fueled violent inmate outbursts and riots such as the incident at Attica in 1971 (Colvin 1992), and massive disparities in both rates of incarceration and access to parole release—particularly with regard to race (Clear et al. 2006; see also Blumstein 1982; Blumstein et al. 1983; C. R. Mann 1993; Pratt 1998; Wilbanks 1987).

Examples of the state behaving badly around this time were certainly not limited to corrections. Diminishing confidence in the government's role in the Vietnam War, the violence associated with the 1968 Democratic National Convention, and the National Guard turning its guns on students at Kent State all served as indicators to justice model liberals that the state cannot be trusted (Cullen and Gilbert 1982). After then offering the phrase "the corruption of benevolence," the justice model camp held that the state is incapable of the fair and effective rehabilitation of offenders (Levrant et al. 1999, 7; see also Griset 1991)—a sentiment that forcefully made its way into popular culture with films such as Stanley Kubrick's *A Clockwork Orange* and Milos Forman's *One Flew Over the Cuckoo's Nest*.

The result of these parallel movements was a system of semideterminate sentences, which transferred discretionary authority over correctional policy to prosecutors, state legislators, and other political entrepreneurs (Eisenstein and Jacob 1977; Marenin 1995; Nardulli, Eisenstein, and Flemming 1988; see also Table 2.1). The expansion in the authority of elected public officials also led to the replacement of rehabilitation-oriented prison wardens with more conservative, punishment-oriented wardens in the mid-1970s (Colvin 1992; J. Jacobs 1977).

These policy changes were also reflected in—and, in part, driven by—a shift in the public consensus about the assumed causes of crime. As Cullen and Gendreau (2000, 112) noted, "the tarnishing of the rehabilitative ideal created opportunities for other ways of 'thinking about crime' to gain ascendancy and to influence the direction of correctional policy." With regard to the justice model liberal camp, the climate of distrust and cynicism toward the government in general in the late 1960s was reflected most clearly in the loss of confidence in the validity of the medical model

Table 2.1 Timeline of Changes in the Social Context, Problem Definition, and Control of Corrections Policy

Time Period	*Social Context*	*Problem Definition*	*Control of Corrections Policy*
Mid-1800s–early 1900s	Laissez-faire capitalism and the minimal state	Moral failing	Religious sphere
Early 1900s–1960s	Modern administrative state	Medical model	Corrections agency professionals
1960s–present	Ideological pluralism with a strong conservative movement	Labeling and coddling of offenders	Policy makers

of offender treatment. It became clear that a host of medical interventions not only failed to effect any long-term behavioral change in inmates, but many of them were also shocking to the conscience. To be sure, prisons had long been laboratories for treatments such as electroshock therapy and risky medical experiments (Mitford 1971), pharmacological cocktails to keep inmates docile (Pratt et al. 1998), and even grinding the testicles of executed offenders into a powder to be consumed by inmates (referred to as "glandular implantation") under the assumption that it would act as a vaccine against violence (see, e.g., Stanley 1940 for claims of this practice's success, not only for reducing violent tendencies among inmates receiving the implantation, but it also apparently helped one inmate "to comprehend jokes" and, in general, to have more "jazz and pep," p. 110). When correctional rehabilitation is associated with such strategies, rehabilitation is bound to get a bad name eventually.

At the same time as the medical model was being rejected by liberal criminologists, a new perspective—labeling theory—was being adopted. According to labeling theorists, crime is amplified when youth are singled out by the criminal justice system and labeled as "delinquents" or "criminals." The label then becomes a self-fulfilling prophecy, or a "master status," which then would lead to even more of the kinds of behaviors that would be congruent with the new criminal identity (Pratt et al. 1998, 456; see also Schur 1971). As such, the policy implications of labeling theory were straightforward. Advocates of this perspective pushed for decarceration (i.e., the reduction of the size of the incarcerated population), diversion, and even what has been termed "radical nonintervention" (Lemert

1967). The doctrine of "least harmful intervention" provided by labeling theory was evident in the juvenile justice reforms in the early 1970s, including the 1974 Juvenile Justice and Delinquency Prevention Act, as well as the earlier Crime Commission reports. The most vivid example was the closing of all juvenile reform schools in Massachusetts in the mid-1970s (J. Miller 1991).

Aside from the rise of labeling theory, however, Blumstein (1997, 353) observed that "the vacuum created by the trashing of rehabilitation was soon to be filled by two other crime control approaches available to the criminal justice system—deterrence and incapacitation" (see also Zimring and Hawkins 1995). Bolstered by the work of economists such as Becker (1968), the classical school of criminology (the rational choice model abandoned in the early 1900s by the positivists) was resuscitated by linking the legal costs of crime to its social costs, such as the loss of respect among loved ones or the loss of employment.

In doing so, criminologists handed political entrepreneurs a silver platter filled with a simple, easy-to-understand "cure" for the crime problem: increase the costs of criminal activity. Rooted in the assumption that would-be offenders are relatively aware of the likelihood of detection and the severity of the penalties for their misbehavior, political figures from the local to the national levels jumped onto the "get tough" bandwagon (Gest 2001). Again, the appeal to policy makers of re-embracing the uncomplicated rational choice view of human behavior was that they were now free to ignore (and to outright dismiss) the possible criminogenic effects of the host of social factors previously implicated as being contributors to crime. Indeed, elected officials were now equipped with the argument that there was no need to continue their attempts to alleviate conditions of economic deprivation in inner-city communities or to devise policies in an effort to combat structured inequalities in our country (see Herrnstein and Murray 1994; Murray 1984; J. Q. Wilson and Herrnstein 1985). Instead, lawmakers can swoop in and save the day with the stroke of a pen by writing new laws that heap harsher penalties upon those who thumb their noses at the law (for a more contemporary version of this position, see Lott 2000).

Political Capital and Getting Tough

The fact that policy makers began to explicitly adopt the "get tough on crime" rhetoric in the late 1960s/early 1970s was no accident. As Gest (2001, 5) noted, "Barry Goldwater started it." In his bid for the 1964 presidency, the Republican candidate from Arizona took what had been previously viewed as a local problem (crime) and put it on the national political agenda. Beginning with his acceptance speech at the Republican National Convention, he promised to make "enforcing law and order" a priority, and in condemning the apparent rise in "violence in the streets," he vowed to "do all that I can to see that women can go out on the streets of the country without being scared stiff" (Cronin, Cronin, and Milakovich 1981, 18). Although Goldwater was crushed in that election by Lyndon Johnson, the Democratic incumbent, Gerald Caplan, the United States Justice Department's crime research chief in the early 1970s, observed that "the effect of Senator Goldwater's lopsided defeat was not to bury crime as an issue, but merely to transfer the official responsibility to the Democratic administration" (1973, 589).

Not to be outdone, key members of the Republican Party continued their attempts to sell their version of the law-and-order message to the American public, and getting (and keeping) crime on the national political agenda proved to be fairly easy. Not only were these efforts quite successful, they also laid the foundation for highlighting the race–crime link that would become the staple of the 1980s war on drugs. Most notably, during his run through the 1968 presidential primaries, Richard Nixon confessed in a letter to former President Dwight Eisenhower that "I have found great audience response to this [law and order] theme in all parts of the country, including areas like New Hampshire where there is virtually no race problem and relatively little crime" (Baum 1996, 11). In addition, as Nixon's White House Chief-of-Staff, Bob Haldeman, noted in his diary, Nixon took the race–crime nexus so seriously that he had informed Haldeman, "you have to face the fact that the whole problem is really the blacks. The key is to devise a system that recognizes this while not appearing to" (Baum 1996, 13).

Thus, with the national leaders of both major political parties shouting the same chorus, the "get tough" game was on, and policy makers at virtually all levels of government seemed willing to play. As time wore on, the appeal of adopting a get-tough stance has almost become a siren song for politicians—luring them in, even perhaps against their better judgment. As a result of our sustained efforts to deal with crime through enhanced punishments, we now have more of our citizens locked up behind bars than the entire population of Kuwait, not to mention another 5 million under some form of community supervision (e.g., federal, state, or local probation and parole supervision; Bureau of Justice Statistics, 2007b).

A problem that has gone largely overlooked by criminologists thus far is the extent to which this growth in our correctional system has been aided by policy makers' use of faulty information about (1) crime, (2) the desires of the American public, and (3) the efficacy of incarceration as a crime control strategy. The three chapters in Part II deal directly with these issues. Although certainly a lofty goal, my hope is that exposing the misinformation perpetuated by the defenders of the get-tough movement will open the door to more honest public debate concerning the harmful consequences (both intended and unintended) of the American state of imprisonment, and that it may boost the political attractiveness of alternative strategies that may be implemented to help us shake the habit of relying so heavily on the quick fix of incarceration.

Note

1. As opposed to thinking about criminal behavior in terms of free will, hedonism, and rationality (the key components of the classical school of criminology), scientific positivism was concerned with uncovering empirical evidence to confirm the notion that crime is the result of multiple (both psychological and sociological) factors.

PART II

This section represents the "meat" of the book and is arguably the most important. Detailed histories of criminal justice policies and practices in general, and corrections in particular, exist elsewhere (Chambliss 1999; Donziger 1996; L. M. Friedman 1993; Gest 2001; Gordon 1990; J. Miller 1996), and even policy discussions associated with the get-tough movement in corrections are not in short supply (Anderson 1998; Austin and Irwin 2001; Clear 1994; Currie 1998; Garland 1990; Mauer 1999; Tonry 1995). Nevertheless, the three chapters contained in this section demonstrate how the policy prescriptions of the last three decades (e.g., mandatory sentences, the "war on drugs," three strikes laws) have been based on three different (yet certainly interrelated) forms of misinformation.

PART II

Three

Misinformation About the Crime Problem

In recent decades, it has become fashionable for political figureheads to decry the nation's "crime problem." News-friendly quips from political pundits come in many flavors, but most often they are merely slight variations of the common theme that crime in the United States is "out of control." Such claims are aided by high-profile violent incidents such as the rise in the number of school shootings—over 20 incidents since 1996, with over 70 deaths and over 100 injured—and the terror brought on by the Washington, D.C.–area snipers in 2002 and the Virginia Tech University shootings in 2007. These events are certainly tragic in their own right, yet they also tap into our deepest fear of crime: stranger-to-stranger violent victimization.

The end result of such tragedies is that policy makers have continued to feel justified in their message to the American citizenry that it is reasonable for all of us to be afraid of the random victimization experienced by those on television since, as evidenced by such horrific events, the crime problem in this country is off the charts. And it is not just crime, but the *kind* of crime—those offenses that citizens buy deadbolts for their doors to shield themselves against—that is important. After all, the message implies, this is not some socially constructed "moral panic" over nothing, but rather a rational response for us to want to protect ourselves from what John DiIulio and colleagues (including former Drug Czar and Department of Education Secretary William Bennett) have dubbed "superpredators"—those intrinsically flawed evildoers who are apparently growing in number (Bennett et al. 1996).

Curiously, this position seems to be at odds with the recent "crime drop" in the United States during the 1990s, which has been described by criminologists as "extraordinary" (Conklin 2003, vii) and "remarkable" (Blumstein and Wallman 2000, 1). Despite this potential call for optimism, some criminologists, such as James Alan Fox (who also frequently appears before Congress on matters of crime policy), still warn us of impending doom: "We are facing a potential bloodbath of teenage violence in years ahead that will be so bad, we'll look back at the 1990s and say those were the good old days" (quoted in Austin and Irwin 2001, 239).[1] Based on comments like this and others like it, DiIulio appeared to make the ongoing exponential growth of the prison system in this country a personal crusade during the 1990s (see, e.g., DiIulio and Piehl 1991). Such growth would be necessary, according to DiIulio (1995, 15), to give us a fighting chance of winning the battle against the "fatherless, Godless, and jobless" superpredators.

This chapter examines the validity of these claims by tracing how three misconceptions about the nature of crime in the United States have served as political fodder for advocates of the expanded use of incarceration. The first misconception is that increases in the "fear of crime" among Americans simply reflect increases in the objective probability of being victimized. This myth is necessary for policy makers to justify the continued growth of incarceration as a means of addressing the fears of their voters. The second misconception is that low-level offenders (e.g., drug and property offenders) will inevitably graduate to violent offending in the absence of a stiff criminal sanction. This erroneous assumption has been the key for stiffening the sanctions associated with virtually all criminal offenses—not just violent crimes. The third misconception is that chronic, life-course persistent offending can be accurately predicted using variables that are given the most "weight" in criminal justice processing: the severity of the offense and the offender's prior record. These factors play directly into enhanced sentencing schemes by being the primary axes for determining an offender's punishment in the sentencing grids that have been adopted by states. By themselves, the acceptance of any one of these mistruths would be enough to cause advocates of mass incarceration to salivate in anticipation and to cause critics of the current state of imprisonment to lose their appetites. When taken together, however, like the combination of heroin and cocaine, these individual slices of misinformation have merged to create a "speedball" political justification for sustaining the incarceration addiction.

Victimization and the Fear of Crime

Prior to the 1960s, crime was not cited by the American public as being a major issue of concern (Chambliss 1999). Even when President Reagan formally launched his "War on Drugs" in 1982—which effectively tied the issues of crime and drugs together for years to come—less than 2 percent of American citizens cited drugs as the nation's most pressing problem. This figure had changed dramatically by the time Reagan's understudy, George Herbert Walker Bush, took office in 1988 (and appointed a "Drug Czar"), at which time 64 percent of Americans believed that the drug problem was the most salient issue facing the nation (Beckett 1997). This trend also followed public concern over crime in general, where even as late as June of 1993—under the leadership of President Bill Clinton this time, and right before Congress began its debate over his "crime bill" proposal—only 7 percent of Americans cited crime as the nation's most important problem. Just 6 months later, and largely as a result of the intense publicity these legislative sessions received, that number had increased to 30 percent (Braun and Pasternak, 1994). By August of 1994, that figure had reached 52 percent, which public opinion pollsters attributed to Clinton's discussion of the crime bill in the State of the Union Address, and to the extensive media coverage of how Congress was considering the bill (Moore 1994; see also Alderman 1994).

It is clear, therefore, that Americans' concern over the crime problem has increased substantially in recent years and, despite stable and even falling crime rates, fear of crime continues to be high (Gallup 1999). As can be seen in Figure 3.1, the trends in American citizens' perceptions of both the crime rates in their local communities and nationally are that crime is not only increasing, but it is doing so dramatically. Even so, these patterns are not new, as Figure 3.2 shows that over the last couple of decades around half of all American citizens have thought that crime is on the rise, regardless of actual changes in rates of criminal behavior. Even in 2002, when the media blitz concerning the crime drop of the 1990s was at its strongest, a quarter of the population still believed that crime rates were increasing. In short, criminal victimization, it turns out, bears a surprisingly inconsistent relationship to fear of victimization (Lewis and Salem 1986; Taylor and Hale 1986; see also Hale 1996). If crime itself does not drive fear of crime, what does?

To answer that question, an understanding of the disconnect between citizens' perceptions of risk and the objective probability of victimization

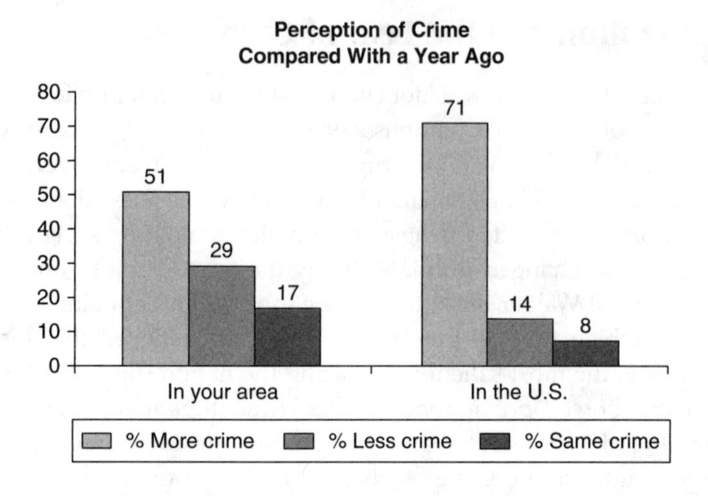

Figure 3.1 Citizens' Perceptions of Local and National Crime Rate Changes

Source: Gallup Poll 2007.

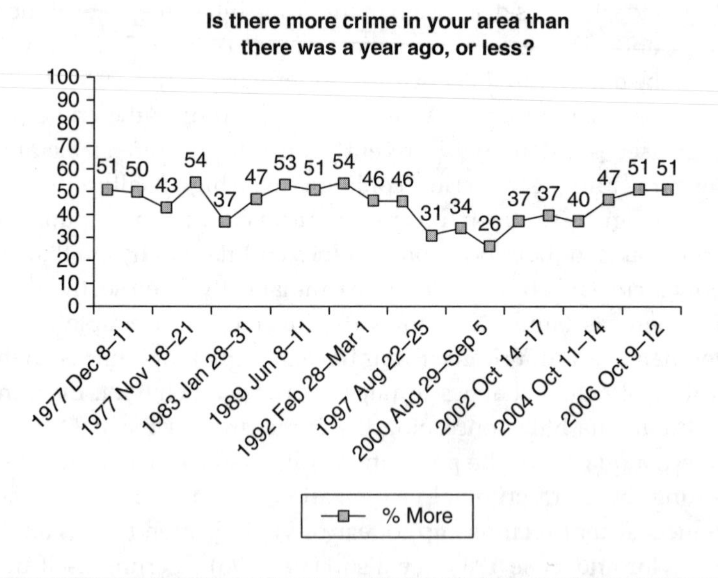

Figure 3.2 Citizens' Perceptions of Local Community Crime Increases From 1977 to 2006

Source: Gallup Poll 2007.

can be reached when it is examined through the lens of school shootings. For example, Brooks, Schiraldi, and Ziedenberg's (2000) analysis of national opinion polls that were taken after the shootings in Jonesboro, Arkansas, and Littleton, Colorado, found a 49 percent increase in parents' anxiety about their children's safety in the classroom. This increase occurred despite studies by the U.S. Department of Justice and the National School Safety Center that showed a 40 percent decrease in school-associated violent deaths in 1998–1999, the school year including the Columbine shooting.

While these violent incidents are undoubtedly serious social problems, their prevalence has been severely blown out of proportion. Although the probability that a child would be the victim of lethal violence in school is 1 in 2 million, an overwhelming majority of parents still feel as though it is likely that a tragic event such as this will occur in their child's school in the future (Bonderman 2001). Misplaced public fear over this issue has even resulted in an increase in the number of kids being homeschooled, presumably in an effort by parents to insulate their children from the inevitable violence that they believe must surely come with going to school with other (unpredictable) youths (Hargrove 2001).

This "knowledge gap" between the reality of crime and the public's perception of that reality is mirrored in the American news media's reliance on crime-related issues to generate advertising revenue. For example, Klite, Bardwell, and Salzman's (1997) survey of 100 television stations found that 72 of them began their evening news programming with a crime story, and that a third of all stories dealt with crime-related issues. Furthermore, Angotti's (1997) study of local news programming in eight major media markets—including the 12 million citizens in New York City's market—found that instances of crime news were twice as common as instances of political news. The reliability of crime stories to attract viewers even led KREM 2 News in Spokane, Washington, to place the phrase "Crime Is Bad" in bold letters across the screen in their 2008 television promotional ads, as if their viewers were unaware of this bit of information and therefore needed to be informed of it.

Put simply, the media have discovered that, in the United States, "crime sells," and Americans are constantly bombarded by images of crime and victimization whenever they turn on their television set or open a newspaper. Nevertheless, some scholars still contend that "media effects" on fear of crime are absent, and have effectively dismissed the existence of a "knowledge gap" outright. For example, J. Young (1987, 337) argued that "popular conceptions of crime . . . are, in the main, constructed out of the material experiences of people, rather than fantasies impressed upon them by mass media." Rubin, Perse, and Taylor (1988, 126) made the similar argument that "television's influence on social reality is overshadowed by direct personal and interpersonal experience" with the reality of crime. Sparks (1992, 2) echoed these sentiments in his contention that "fear is so plainly a product of the real conditions of existence . . . as to leave no space for the role of the mass media in accounting for it."

Statements like these perpetuate the misconception that citizens' fear of crime is a natural consequence of their objective probability of victimization and that the media does nothing to elevate levels of fear beyond one's own personal experiences. The fundamental problem with these arguments, however, is that they are based merely on speculation as opposed to solid, social scientific evidence. Recent empirical work on criminal victimization and the fear of crime sheds light on the myth that American citizens' fear of crime—which has been used to justify the prison boom in recent decades—is solely a function of their own immediate experiences.

Media Influences on Fear of Crime

The relationship between media influences and fear of crime has been well studied (see reviews by Eschholz 1997; Heath and Gilbert 1996). Only three studies of this relationship, however, have been conducted using data more recent than 1981—the time at which rapid prison expansion began. Furthermore, studies rarely differentiate between local and national news media effects (for an exception, see Barzagan 1994). Finally, no studies have included controls for the crime rate (as a measure of the "reality" of crime), and studies that do control for the effect of personal victimization on fear of crime (see Chiricos, Eschholz, and Gertz 1997) have been limited to single communities.

In an effort to address these methodological shortcomings, Chiricos, Padgett, and Gertz (2000) have conducted the most rigorous study of the effect of television news content on citizens' fear of crime to date. In a statewide survey of Florida residents, they isolated the independent effect of news media programming (both local and national) on fear of crime by controlling for citizens' prior victimization experiences and even their perception of the level of safety in their neighborhood. Their results indicated that, even after controlling for such experiences, exposure to both local and national news media sources significantly increased citizens' fear of crime. These effects are even more telling when the magnitude—or "strength of effects"—is taken into account. In particular, the magnitude of the media effects (local and national combined) on fear of crime was nearly twice as large as the effect of personal victimization experiences on fear of crime. These results therefore suggest that American citizens' fear of crime, while to a certain extent rooted in personal experience, is to a greater degree determined by their level of exposure to the spectacle of human horrors depicted by news media organizations.

Linking Fear to Leniency

Beckett's (1997) analysis of national public opinion surveys from 1964 to 1992 also found that changes in public concern over crime (which included indicators of concern over drugs) were unrelated to changes in crime rates. Like Chiricos and colleagues (2000), Beckett found that public concern was instead predicted by media coverage of issues associated with crime and drugs. Furthermore, and perhaps more important, public concern about crime over time was most closely tied to what she referred to as "political initiative," which is defined as "the number of speeches, statements, policy initiatives, or summaries pertaining to crime . . . made by federal officials and reported in the mass media" (1997, 116).

After placing the crime issue at the top of the political agenda, policy makers—abetted by a willing media—were then able to cultivate the public's fear of crime. Even so, as stated in Chapter 1, throwing gasoline on the fear fire was not enough, by itself, to justify a dramatic increase in prison population growth. To do that, policy makers needed to frame the apparent crime problem as a consequence of excessive leniency on the part of the criminal justice system—the techniques for which have been honed to perfection by political elites over the last 30 years. It is clear, however, that their ability to do so has been predicated on misinformation about the degree to which citizens' fears about being victimized are driven by their own experiences versus the lurid images of crime and victimization they are flooded with on a regular basis. In short, our state of mass incarceration cannot be justified on the basis that it is necessary to allay the portion of citizens' fear of crime that can be attributed to instances of personal victimization since such experiences have little to do with fear of crime.

Nonserious Crime as Gateway Offending?

In 1981, Nancy Reagan's advisors sought to change her image from a china-buying White House decorator to something with more political substance. Determined not to be stuck in some budgetary role or in some policy job (after all, these were tasks tackled by her predecessors), Mrs. Reagan informed her projects director that she wanted to address the issue of "drug abuse" (see Baum 1996, 141). Despite the warnings from the media-savvy Communications Director Michael Deaver—who instead suggested focusing on something "fun" along the lines of volunteerism or historic preservation—Nancy went forth with the drug abuse issue. What followed was the memorable "just say no" antidrug campaign, which spawned a number of subsequent generations of antidrug television spots, from "parents who use drugs have children who use drugs" (recall the defiant youth shouting at his father, "You, alright? I learned it by watching you!") to the father figure in the kitchen cracking eggs into a bacon grease–filled cast iron pan who says, "this is your brain; this is your brain on drugs." To push the "just say no" message a step further, Mrs. Reagan even made a cameo appearance alongside Gary Coleman on the television comedy *Diff'rent Strokes* in a storyline about drug use among school-aged children.

The underlying theme of the antidrug movement throughout the 1980s was not simply that drug use, in and of itself, is harmful. Rather, the message being sent to kids and, more importantly, to their parents, was that drug use is a type of "gateway offense" that opens the door to the full spectrum of criminal behavior for youths. Rising levels of violent offending during the 1980s, which were often linked to inner-city drug markets by the media and by political entrepreneurs, led the public and policy makers to adopt a misconception about the "escalation" of the severity of offending by individuals.[2] Specifically, the political culture surrounding crime—especially since the early 1980s—makes the implicit assumption that if someone is committing low-level offenses now (such as drug abuse or theft), it is only a matter of time until the person graduates into committing violent offenses such as robbery, rape, and murder. It is my contention here that this concern is misplaced, and that it is inconsistent with the reality of criminal-offending trajectories.

Categorical Contagion

The image of a young punk stealing someone's bike does not generally cause people to go and buy state-of-the-art alarm systems for their houses, to clip cans of pepper spray to their key rings, or to avoid walking home alone in the dark. These types of reactions are instead attributed to the fear of violent victimization, especially the threat of lethal violence, which is the major source of fear and anxiety for Americans. Of course, the fear of lethal violence is not unique to Americans. Kristof (1996) notes that the fear of gunshot wounds is even quite prevalent among Japanese citizens, despite the fact that there were only 32 gun-related homicides in 1995 (roughly half of the total for Newark, New Jersey, in any given year). But the United States does experience a higher rate of homicide victimization than any other Western industrialized nation (Pratt and Godsey 2003), so American citizens' fears of being murdered, in particular, are not necessarily unfounded relative to citizens of other nations. What *is* uniquely American, however, is that our fear of lethal violence has spread like a virus into a universal fear of all forms of crime—even those that pose no credible threat to our physical safety.

Zimring and Hawkins (1997, 13) referred to this phenomenon as "categorical contagion," which they defined as "the agency whereby citizens come to fear many forms of criminal behavior because they imagine them all committed by extremely violent protagonists." Even some criminologists, such as James Q. Wilson and George Kelling (1982), have perpetuated this pattern of overgeneralization in their argument that low-level instances of incivility and disorder in a community will inexorably lead to direct, violent, predatory victimization in the absence of some formal intervention.[3] In short, today's thief or burglar is tomorrow's rapist and killer. Yet, if this is true, why do we not find the same level and quality of fear of crime among citizens living in nations where the rate of property offending is comparable to ours, such as the United Kingdom? If there really is some sort of "law of escalation" in the severity of offending, fear of crime should be directly commensurate with the supply of potential criminal offenders in any given social context.

Upon closer examination, this proposition simply does not hold up. There is no credible empirical evidence of a progression of increasing severity in the offenses committed over the length of a criminal career (Shannon 1991; Wolfgang, Figlio, and Sellin 1972). On the one hand, offenders—even chronic offenders—are quite versatile in their offending patterns (i.e., they generally are not too picky about which offense to commit when the opportunities to do so are easy; see Piquero, Farrington, and Blumstein 2003). Nevertheless, recent work based on a large sample of high-risk, persistent offenders found no evidence of either offending "specialization" in violence or of systematic escalation of lower-level offending (e.g., drug and property offending) to violent personal crimes (McGloin et al. 2007; C. J. Sullivan et al. 2006). In short, the evidence suggests that although offenders may exhibit a lot of bad behavior, we have no reason to believe that engaging in more mundane misbehavior will, by definition, lead to the kinds of serious violent offending that tend to *really* scare people.

To illustrate this point, Zimring and Hawkins (1997) noted that for every 10 theft offenses reported in Sydney, Australia, there are just over 13 reported in Los Angeles, and for every 10 burglaries reported in Sydney, there are 9 in Los Angeles. Thus, it appears as though the overall supply of criminal offenders is roughly the same across the two cities. As stated in Chapter 1, however, for every 100 homicides in Los Angeles, there are only 4.8 in Sydney. It is clear, therefore, that (1) despite comparable numbers of potential offenders, the nature of crime differs considerably across these two communities, and (2) a general fear of "crime" has little to do with crime at all, but rather with lethal violence, which, again, is a condition somewhat unique unto itself in the United States.

Implications for Corrections Policy

The problem is that this categorical contagion has had major implications for prison growth in this country. Here lies the fundamental paradox: as states create stiffer sanctions—presumably in an effort to rid the streets of those who would commit acts of life-threatening violence—the bulk of enforcement efforts will typically be directed toward *nonserious offenders.* Even before the creation of baseball metaphor–enhanced sentencing policies such as "Three Strikes and You're Out," offenses such as armed robbery, aggravated sexual assault, and murder almost always resulted in a prison sentence. Even with limited prison space, we can always find a bed for folks like Jeffrey Dahmer, Ted Bundy, and Gary Ridgeway (the infamous "Green River Killer"). As prison space expands, who are we going to fill prison cells with if we are already locking up serious violent offenders?

The answer, of course, is nonserious offenders. Austin and Irwin's (2001) analysis of prison admissions confirms this recent trend. Their work indicates that the most frequent crime resulting in a prison sentence is drug possession (22 percent), which is followed by burglary (20 percent), theft and fraud (20 percent), and drug delivery (15 percent), and that these four nonviolent crimes constitute 77 percent of all prison admissions. It is therefore quite obvious that in our efforts to round up violent offenders, a sizeable portion of nonviolent—and nonserious—offenders have been caught in the net. This has resulted in a dramatic shift in the composition of the inmate population in this country. What we have now is a rather large gap between violence and imprisonment—one that is aided, at least in part, by the third misconception about crime in America: that we can accurately predict whether someone is likely to be a chronic, life-course persistent offender by taking into account the severity of his or her current offense and the extent of the person's prior record of offending.

Incapacitation and Errors in Prediction

The notion of incapacitation as a legitimate goal of punishment—incarcerating an offender so that he or she cannot break the law, at least for the duration of the individual's stay in prison—is a recent phenomenon in American correctional policy. The problem in the past has been that we believed that through imprisonment, some sort of "incapacitation effect" was inevitable (and therefore theoretically uninteresting), which contributed to incapacitation's status as a secondary purpose of punishment at best (Zimring and Hawkins 1995). In essence, incapacitation suffered from the "no duh" syndrome, where lawmakers knew they would get a marginal incapacitation effect through the incarceration of offenders. The risk of focusing on this potential benefit, however, seemed to come at the cost of admitting to the failure of both rehabilitation- and deterrence-based correctional philosophies (Feeley and Simon 1992; see also Pratt and Cullen 2005).

This all changed with Wolfgang et al.'s (1972) "birth cohort" study of Philadelphia youth, which found that 6 percent of the kids in their cohort were responsible for over half of the arrests or police contacts—a finding that has been replicated rather consistently in subsequent research (see, e.g., Chaiken and Chaiken 1984; Shannon 1991; J. D. Wright and Rossi 1986). To lawmakers in the 1970s and 1980s (see J. Q. Wilson 1975), the policy implications of this body of research were as clear as could be: since most criminal offenses are committed by a small proportion of the offender population, crime rates could be substantially reduced if we could lock up those "high-rate" offenders before they embark on their lifelong pattern of criminal activity.

Selective Incapacitation

Like any sexy policy proposal, this concept was given a catchy name to help it resonate with policy makers and the American public: "selective incapacitation." To assess the potential social value of a selective incapacitation strategy, the National Institute of Justice funded a multisite, longitudinal study of "criminal careers"—the result of which was a study published by the Rand Corporation in 1982 (Greenwood and Abrahamse 1982). Using a sample of inmates convicted of robbery and burglary from three states (Texas, Michigan, and California), Greenwood and Abrahamse constructed a seven-factor predictive scale that was composed largely of items tapping into an offender's prior criminal history (e.g., prior convictions and incarcerations, age at first conviction, substance abuse).[4] Using items such as these was critical for the successful implementation of the selective incapacitation model, since information about these factors is easily accessible to prosecutors and judges—the primary "players" in the sentencing process. Put simply, the selective incapacitation model is only seductive for policy makers if it is fairly easy to predict (with easily obtainable information) whether a particular offender will be a career criminal.

To determine if this is so, Greenwood and Abrahamse (1982) correlated their predictive scale with the self-reported estimates of offending from the inmates in their sample. Based on their analyses, they concluded that their predictive scale is accurate enough at identifying high-rate offenders that it should be used during the sentencing decision. More specifically, the high-rate offenders identified by the predictive scale should receive longer sentences so that the maximum benefit to public safety (crime reduction) could be achieved. By that same token, low-level offenders, as identified by the same predictive scale, should be given shorter sentences in order to maximize the efficient use of finite correctional resources.

It is simple to see why this model for corrections policy became so popular. The idea of reducing crime by locking people up for an extended period of time—as opposed to wasting our energy trying to change offenders' behavior through rehabilitative practices—was consistent with the social and political climate of the 1970s and 1980s. Thus, such a policy proposal "made sense" in the social context of the time. The conservative shift in correctional ideology during this time was even powerful enough to cause policy makers—as well as their constituents—to ignore the ethical and due process concerns associated with a selective incapacitation strategy. In particular, the selective incapacitation framework *punishes offenders for crimes that have yet to be committed*—a practice that legal scholars generally denounce as being inconsistent with the basic precepts of justice and the foundation of American criminal law (Packer 1968; von

Hirsch 1984, 1985; see also Dworkin 1985). As problematic as this may be, such ethical concerns ended up playing second fiddle to the proposed public safety benefits of selective incapacitation, especially since "rigorous social scientific research" had clearly demonstrated that the identification of high-rate offenders is both practical and possible, and that it does not require the detailed knowledge of each offender's battery of social and psychological factors.

Errors in Prediction: False Positives

Like any human endeavor—from forecasting the weather to guessing someone's age—predicting who will be a high-rate offender will come with a certain degree of error. In the context of selective incapacitation, one kind of error is the "false negative," where some decision rule (perhaps Greenwood and Abrahamse's predictive scale) labels someone as low or medium risk when he or she is actually a high-rate offender. Should this offender receive a shorter sentence on the basis of the person's designated risk level under a selective incapacitation sentencing scheme, there may be an enhanced risk to public safety if that offender is released into the community too early.

Although this issue is certainly important, the corollary problem of "false positives" has been of greater concern for researchers and policy makers interested in constructing a rational and efficient sentencing system, as well as for advocates of due process and fair sentencing practices, where there is a heightened concern that incarceration resources should be judiciously reserved for the worst of the worst criminal offenders. In this case, the errors come in the form of "overprediction," where low- (or medium-) risk offenders are erroneously predicted to be chronic, high-rate offenders. Again, given that selective incapacitation involves extending the period of incarceration for an individual according to offenses not yet committed, the problem of false positives means that we may be locking people up for crimes that they probably would not commit anyway. This definitely raises ethical and due process concerns, but the practical downfall of the existence of false positives is that correctional resources are squandered on people who have been incorrectly identified, thus raising the costs of incarceration for public budgets that are already stretched to the limit.

This problem would be moot, however, if the rate of accurate identification to risk-level categories was high—as claimed by Greenwood and

Abrahamse (1982). Unfortunately, nothing could be further from the truth. In fact, one might be surprised that, although we can predict with a certain measure of confidence that a small proportion of offenders in any given community will be career criminals (or high-rate offenders), our success rate for predicting just *who* those folks will be at the individual level is truly dismal. Even Blumstein, Cohen, and Farrington (1988), some of the most respected experts in criminal career research, each of whom had access to information on a host of personal, social, and environmental characteristics of offenders, readily confessed to the inability to identify chronic criminal "persisters" until they were already well into their criminal careers (see also Petersilia 1980).

The problem gets even worse when we start looking at the error rates associated with the purported predictive scale offered by Greenwood and Abrahamse (1982) themselves. Specifically, their analysis indicates an overall success rate of only 51 percent in correctly classifying criminal offenders. Their false positive rate—where offenders are incorrectly classified as high-risk—is 48 percent, and reanalyses of the same Rand data conducted by J. Cohen (1983) and by Visher (1986) placed that figure even higher, at 55 percent. Perhaps the most damaging blow to the selective incapacitation argument came with Auerhahn's (1999) replication of Greenwood and Abrahamse's work on a sample of California inmates. Not only did she continue to find relatively low (yet slightly better) overall predictive accuracy at 60 percent, her results also indicated serious problems with the reliability of the original Greenwood and Abrahamse predictive scale. For example, various items contained in the predictive scale—all of which purportedly tap into the same dimension of "seriousness"—were, at best, only weakly related to one another. In other words, knowing how someone scored on one dimension of the scale (e.g., substance abuse) provides little insight into how he or she will score on another dimension of the scale (e.g., age at first arrest).

In the end, the lure of selective incapacitation as a strategy for corrections policy rests on the assumption that we can identify high-rate offenders in a prospective manner, and that we can do so early enough in each offender's criminal career that we can get the largest potential reduction in crime for our correctional dollar by throwing such miscreants in prison for lengthy periods of time. The problem is that no credible social scientific evidence exists that indicates this can be done. Our inability to correctly identify who among our offender population will come to resemble

Wolfgang et al.'s (1972) "chronic 6 percenters" does not exactly conjure up images of Nostradamus; it instead tends to evoke the more arbitrary image of a coin flip. Regardless of the metaphor, so long as political pundits continue to boast about the potential incapacitative effects of enhanced sentencing policies, they can only do so by ignoring the fact that such claims are based on faulty assumptions regarding the ability of a few criminal history variables to predict complex human behavior over the life course.

Summary

The purpose of this chapter was not to trivialize the issue of crime—especially violent crime and the fear that it engenders—in the United States. To be sure, our rates of violent interpersonal offending are well above those of our Western industrialized peer nations, particularly our levels of homicide victimization. Decision makers in the policy and media arenas have taken this unfortunate reality, however, and have stretched, nipped, and tucked it so much that the face of truth about crime in America is barely recognizable.

This might not be such a problem if the systematic distortion of information was used solely for entertainment purposes. Obviously, this is not the case. Beckett and Sasson's (2003) recent work highlights how receptive Americans are to such misinformation with the popularity of reality TV programming such as *Cops* and *To Catch a Predator.* Nevertheless, political entrepreneurs (and their media sidekicks) have methodically used misinformation about why Americans are so fearful of crime, about patterns of escalation in the seriousness of offenders' criminal careers, and about our ability to predict long-term chronic criminal behavior over the life course with a few simple variables, in an effort to gain political capital.

What we are left with is a caricature of the picture of our current crime problem, complete with exaggerated features that American citizens now consider the "real thing." The purpose of this chapter, therefore, was to highlight how various pieces of misinformation about the crime problem in this country have been used by policy makers to support initiatives—such as the war on drugs and all forms of enhanced sentencing policies—that have fueled our dependence on the incarceration "solution" to the crime problem.

Notes

1. It is worth noting that other criminologists, although not quite as zealous as Fox, also caution against the blatant "triumphalism" (see Currie 1999, 3) of those claiming credit for the crime drop of the 1990s. What may seem like an extreme downward swing in crime rates may just be part of a larger trend of reestablishing an equilibrium following unusually high levels of crime in the 1980s (see also J. J. Donohue 1998; W. Friedman 1998; LaFree 1998).

2. It is important to note that increases in violent crime during this time period were, in fact, highly correlated with patterns of drug use, drug distribution, and gang violence (B. Johnson, Golub, and Dunlap 2000). The problem, however, comes when policy makers cling to the false assumption—and claim publicly—that the social processes that lead to the problems of drug use and gang violence are somehow independent of those that influence rates of violent crime. In short, one set of problems (drugs and gang violence) cannot "cause" another problem (violent crime) if the two emerge from a common source (e.g., concentrated disadvantage in urban communities; see W. J. Wilson 1987).

3. Despite its popularity among police agencies and policy makers, the notion that low levels of disorder actually cause an increase in more severe forms of crime has yet to receive much in the way of serious empirical support (see the discussion in Harcourt 2001). Instead, the social scientific evidence on the subject attributes serious crime to social conditions that lead to both disorder and crime (i.e., disorder cannot cause crime since the two are both consequences of the same social processes; see Sampson 2006; Sampson and Raudenbush 1999). Moreover, recent evidence also suggests that citizens do not even make a mental distinction between their perceptions of disorder and of crime (Gau and Pratt, forthcoming), which lends further evidence to the categorical contagion thesis.

4. Only one item in Greenwood and Abrahamse's (1982) predictive scale was not related to prior offending history: whether the offender had been employed less than 50 percent in the preceding 2 years.

Four

Misinformation About Public Opinion

In the corner of northeastern Washington State, Stevens County residents take their property rights seriously—particularly those who live in the more rural areas of the county (which itself does not contain any urban territory as defined by the U.S. Census Bureau). One citizen, whose address is well off the paved road where the nearest "neighbor" is over a mile away, has interpreted property rights in a way that apparently trumps the Criminal Code of Washington, with a hand-painted plywood sign beside his driveway that reads "Traspassers [sic] will be shot."

And he is not alone. Another instance of a citizen attempting to establish law via a painted-plywood announcement took place in a southern state, where an off-duty police officer, who was traveling along a rural dirt road, came across a hand-painted sign reading "Meth for Sale." While initially skeptical that someone would be foolish enough to advertise his or her criminal activity so boldly (was this merely a joke?), the officer decided to take a look anyway. It turned out that, yes, the gentleman was, in fact, exercising his entrepreneurial talents and was in the business of methamphetamine production and distribution; he was subsequently arrested.[1] Apparently, there is among the American public sufficient ignorance of legislative dynamics and constitutional jurisprudence that certain citizens feel as though the presence of a homemade sign constitutes enough legal protection to sell meth and to shoot people who trespass.

These true tales of misunderstanding of the basics of the legal process may come as no surprise to academics, a group with a rather long history of lamenting American citizens' lack of knowledge of public policy issues in general. Those who contend that the "depth of ignorance" is "breathtaking" (Kinder 1998, 785) and that the "fundamental public ignorance of the central facts of political life" is pervasive (Neuman 1986, 14), need not look too far for obvious examples (like those above) to support such claims. To name just a few, researchers have found that a sizable majority of Americans could not come up with the name of their representative to the U.S. House of Representatives, nor did they know the length of the terms served by U.S. Senators (Kinder 1998). And despite President George W. Bush's New Haven, Connecticut birth and his private education in the Northeast, many Americans still believe that he was born and raised a Texan (Sheehy, 2000).

When it comes to public knowledge about the realities of crime and punishment, things are not much different. One the one hand, there is evidence that the American public is generally cognizant of broad trends in certain types of serious crime (Warr 1980, 1982). On the other hand, when researchers get into the details, the public gets a little tripped up. In particular, research indicates that citizens are chronically ignorant with regard to issues such as variations in violent crime rates over time, the recidivism rates of those coming out of prison or other forms of supervision, the extent of due process protections afforded to defendants in criminal case processing, and the extent to which certain criminal defenses—such as the insanity defense—are used successfully (see Roberts 1992; Roberts and Stalans 1997). Public knowledge becomes even murkier when it gets into sentencing options for offenders, where citizens may not even know what sentencing alternatives can be imposed (aside from incarceration, such as probation or intensive supervision) and, even if such alternatives to imprisonment can be handed out, what these community supervision options actually entail (Hough and Roberts 1999). According to Roberts and Stalans (1997), the general trend indicates that Americans consistently underestimate the severity of sentences that actually get imposed on offenders.

Public opinion researchers have long held that this state of affairs is understandable—perhaps even rational (Kinder 1998). Specifically, Cullen et al. (2000, 4) noted that, given the busy lives of Americans and the seemingly endless roster of policy issues about which one would need to become well versed—not just crime, but education, health care, social security, national defense, taxation, immigration, the environment, and so on—the opportunity costs of being a "political junky" are unacceptably high for most citizens. In short, for the typical "overworked American" (Schor 1992), the dream of being a "policy buff"—while potentially great in theory—is easily squashed under the time-crunching weight of day-to-day routines.

Despite this rather obvious presence of ignorance about the realities of crime and punishment, some criminal justice policy pundits have argued that the absence of such knowledge on the part of the public is irrelevant. What is instead important are the wishes of the American public about what should be done about the crime problem. On that front, punitive punishment policy advocates have been rather clear. For example, DiIulio (1997, 2) has contended that "with respect to crime control, all that Americans have ever demanded from government, and all that they have been demanding since the mid-1960s, are commonsense policies that result in the detection, arrest, conviction, and punishment of violent and repeat criminals." In extending this statement to all types of lawbreakers—not just violent or repeat offenders—DiIulio went on to argue that, in particular, American citizens want incarceration-based policies "that do not return persons who assault, rape, rob, burglarize, *deal drugs,* and murder to the streets without regard to public safety" (emphasis added).

Such statements assume two things, the first of which is that the American public is unilaterally punitive in what types of crime control policies it considers acceptable—most notably, get-tough (or tougher) "lock 'em up" strategies. Second, and even more disturbing, DiIulio's characterization of American public opinion seems to indicate that citizens are incapable of having a complex thought about a complex policy arena, especially when discussing what should be done about violent versus nonviolent offenders. Only by making these assumptions can policy makers' continued reliance on incarceration as the primary tool for controlling crime be justified on the grounds of simply translating public sentiment into public policy.

But would corrections policy makers be so willing to embrace the gamut of stiffer penalties in the face of evidence that American citizens' views on crime and punishment are actually more flexible and judicious than they are thoughtless and unyielding (see Thomson and Ragona 1987)? Upon pulling together public opinion data from a number of diverse areas, Cullen et al. (2000, 6) concluded that "public opinion, while clearly punitive in important ways, nonetheless is progressive in equally important ways." This notion is elaborated more fully in this chapter, which discusses the role of misinformation about Americans' opinions on crime, criminal justice, and punishment in the context of our contemporary imprisonment binge.

In this chapter, research will be reviewed demonstrating that Americans' views on crime and punishment are far more complex than policy makers want to admit. While Americans do harbor fairly punitive "global" opinions about crime and the use of incarceration, a number of recent studies have shown that when it gets to the "specifics," Americans also support the philosophy and practice of correctional rehabilitation (as opposed to the more hard-nosed deterrence and incapacitation approaches), early intervention strategies with juveniles, and alternatives to incarceration for nonserious drug and property offenders. The broad point of this chapter is that policy makers have outpaced the desire of the American public to increase the punitiveness of punishment policies. The current state of incarceration in the United States is therefore due, in part, to policy makers' opportunistic use of misinformation regarding Americans' opinions about crime and punishment.

Global Versus Specific Attitudes About Punishment

Assessing public opinion on a straightforward issue such as who American citizens would want to win the World Series in a given year has never been much of a challenge for pollsters. Accurately summarizing public opinion on this subject is easy since the spectrum of preferences is bound to be rather narrow—for example, either you're pulling for the New York Yankees or you're not (especially if the sample of citizens is drawn from Boston, where Red Sox fans' animosity for the dreaded Yanks dates back to the early 1900s). Given the plurality of individuals' value systems and personal experiences concerning the issues associated with crime and punishment, however, citizens' opinions about these subjects are likely to be more multifaceted.

Researchers have squabbled among each other about what the appropriate method for assessing public opinion should be (see, e.g., Biemer et al. 1991; Muircheartaigh 1997; Roberts 1992; Roberts and Stalans 1997; Schuman and Presser 1981). In the end, most punishment-related polls have been conducted via telephone surveys that ask one or two questions of individuals—many of which merely require a simple yes or no answer (e.g., "Do you think Three-Strikes-and-You're-Out laws are a good thing?" or "Are you in favor of mandatory minimum sentences?"). This methodological approach can be enormously useful in many ways. Since the same questions can be asked repeatedly over time, we can examine trends in public opinion over the years (e.g., are Americans becoming more or less punitive?). These studies also have the advantage in that the samples drawn for these polls are often nationally representative, which allows researchers to generalize their findings to the nation as a whole. They can even be put into action quickly when a hot-button policy issue splashes onto the scene (e.g., capital punishment for juveniles involved in school shooting incidents).

Despite these potential advantages, it is possible that this methodological approach has contributed to our misunderstanding of how Americans actually feel about punishment. Put differently, public attitudes about punishment may very well change under certain conditions (e.g., public preferences for incarceration for first-time offenders versus habitual criminals; community supervision for drug offenders versus violent offenders; the appropriate sentence for impoverished versus affluent offenders). Thus, polls that ask only a couple of questions are incapable of tapping into that level of complexity and may therefore overestimate the degree to which the public actually harbors such punitive beliefs about what should be done with lawbreakers.

Global Attitudes About Punishment

"Global" attitudes about punishment—again, those that are tapped into most often by public opinion polls—are people's general opinions when asked about a particular policy issue. When it comes to global attitudes about punishment, the existing data clearly point to a punitive American public. To illustrate this point, a number of polls have indicated that over 70 percent of Americans are in favor of the death penalty (see Cullen et al. 2000; Longmire 1996), and substantial support for capital punishment has even been found for offenders who do not murder, but who have instead been convicted of armed robbery, residential burglary, or child molestation. Even more telling are the Gallup poll data showing that citizens are still supportive of capital punishment even if it means that innocent people might get executed (see the discussion in Unnever and Cullen 2005; Moore 1995).

These attitudes extend well beyond the issue of capital punishment. Since 1972, the General Social Survey (GSS) has asked the following question: "In general, do you think the courts in this area deal too harshly or not harshly enough with criminals?" In 1972, a total of 65 percent of respondents said "not harsh enough." That figure jumped to 78 percent only 2 years later, and has since hovered above the 80 percent mark (Maguire and Pastore 1998; T. W. Smith 1998). Subsequent national polls indicate that these results are not limited to the GSS. A 1996 CBS News poll, for example, revealed that "to solve the country's crime problem," 54 percent selected the use of "stricter sentences"—a mark more than twice as large as the percentage choosing "increase police" (at 26 percent).

When it comes to the question of how we should fix the "crime problem," Americans' global attitudes are once again clear: abandon our faithful allegiance to leniency (whether it be real or imagined) and increase the use of incarceration for longer periods of time and for more types of offenders (Jacoby and Cullen 1998; Rossi and Berk 1997; Rossi, Berk, and Campbell 1997; Warr 1995). The most reasonable conclusion that could be reached after a review of the studies of global attitudes is that Americans are generally a punitive bunch, and that we like the idea that policies designed to increase our use of prisons can control crime. Given these preferences, it is not surprising how policy makers have used these global attitudes to justify the continued growth and maintenance of our current state of incarceration.

Specific Attitudes About Punishment

The problem with studies that take the "global attitudes" route has nothing to do with what they find. Make no mistake about it: the general punitiveness of the American public is no methodological artifact. The problem is that, with such a limited set of survey items, a host of more specific—and potentially illuminating—questions about citizens' punishment attitudes never get asked. This omission is critically important since research suggests that citizens' sentencing preferences differ once they are provided with information regarding the circumstances of the offense and the offender, and when survey respondents are given a host of sentencing alternatives to incarceration from which to choose (e.g., community supervision, treatment programs; see Cullen et al. 2000). As a couple of examples to highlight this point, let us look more closely at the research assessing citizens' "specific" attitudes about "Three-Strikes-and-You're-Out" policies (for which there is considerable "global" opinion support) and the use of sentencing alternatives to incarceration for offenders.

Three Strikes and You're Out

A study conducted by Applegate, Cullen, Turner, et al. (1996) of Cincinnati residents found that nearly 90 percent of respondents harbored "global" attitudes in favor of "three strikes" policies. Like previous research on the subject, these attitudes emerged out of a response to a single question concerning whether those sampled do or do not support a sentence of life in prison for offenders with two felonies on their prior record who have been convicted of a third serious felony.

This level of support for the three strikes policy of life in prison dwindled considerably, however, when respondents were provided with sample "vignettes" (or scenarios) that contained randomly distributed characteristics of the context of the third felony offense (e.g., detailed descriptions of different offender and offense types). Given this added information—along with a host of potential sentencing options *other* than life in prison from which to choose the appropriate sanction—only a tiny minority of respondents still stuck to their original punitive guns. Only a mere 7 percent still recommended a life sentence without the possibility of parole.

Most of the "exceptions" citizens made to the three strikes policy had to do with the nature of the third felony offense, where more lenient sentences were advocated for those offenders with a nonviolent third offense, or who may not pose a threat to the community (e.g., those convicted of property offenses such as theft or who may be amenable to substance abuse treatment). Given the degree to which citizens change their minds about their punishment preferences when more information is provided to them, Applegate, Cullen, Turner, et al. (1996, 528) concluded that "it does not appear that most citizens wish to implement three-strikes legislation that is blind to specific circumstances and prohibits discretion in sentencing offenders to lifetime incarceration." It is also noteworthy that such a finding is not idiosyncratic to this single study. The trend toward more reasoned and balanced punishment preferences once specific attitudes are tapped has consistently been found across a number of studies (Applegate et al. 2000; Applegate, Cullen, Turner, et al. 1996; Doble, Immerwahr, and Richardson 1991; Doble and Klein 1989; Keil and Vito 1991; Sandys and McGarrell 1995; Unnever and Cullen 2005; Unnever, Roberts, and Cullen 2005).

Alternatives to Incarceration

Consistent with the findings regarding citizens' punishment preferences for three strikes laws, a large body of research also points to a high level of public support for sanctions other than incarceration, even for potentially serious offenders (Anderson 1998; Harlow, Darley, and Robinson 1995; Turner et al. 1997). Much of this public support is aimed at correctional programs that fall under the heading of "intermediate sanctions." The intellectual seeds of most of these programs were planted in the 1960s in an effort to provide judges with sanction options other than prison and standard probation (Fulton et al. 1997; Petersilia and Turner 1990). A short list of these programs includes intensive supervision probation/ parole (ISP), boot camps (also known as shock incarceration programs), electronic monitoring/home confinement, fines, day reporting centers, residential community programs, and community service (Byrne, Lurigio, and Petersilia 1992; Renzema 1992; Watts and Glaser 1992; see also Cullen, Wright, and Applegate 1996).

What made these programs eventually flourish—especially in the 1980s—was that they were politically attractive to policy stakeholders on both ends of the ideological spectrum. Liberals liked them because they held the potential to keep certain offenders (e.g., nonviolent offenders) out of prison; conservatives, on the other hand, liked them because they contained the promise of a stiffer sanction than probation for certain deserving offenders (Morris and Tonry 1990). Yet despite the popularity of these programs among policy makers, much of the public remains frighteningly unaware of their existence (Hough and Roberts 1999). Public opinion polls limited to global assessments of citizens' punishment proclivities are therefore unable to gauge the degree to which citizens may endorse such programs. When respondents to opinion polls are given the option of sentencing particular offenders, under particular situations, to an array of intermediate sanctions (as opposed to prison), we once again see how uncovering specific attitudes highlights the misconception that Americans are mindlessly punitive.

For example, studies have shown that the public overwhelmingly supports the use of a host of intermediate sanctions, especially for nonviolent offenders[2]—those comprising the largest portion of our current inmate population (Brown and Elrod 1995; Elrod and Brown 1996; Flanagan 1996; Reichel and Gauthier 1990; Senese 1992). Even further, research has indicated that, given the opportunity, survey respondents will often tailor their preferred sentences to the specific traits of individual offenders (e.g., drug treatment programs for offenders with alcohol/substance abuse problems; boot camp facilities for those convicted of burglary; see Doble Research Associates 1995a, b, c).

The degree of public support for alternatives to incarceration is even more pronounced in studies that inform respondents of the relative costs associated with an array of intermediate sanctions (Doble and Klein 1989; Doble et al. 1991; Farkas 1993; G. Jacobs 1993). The result of this approach is that exposure to such knowledge—which again taps into domains of "specific" attitudes—has a profound impact on citizens' punishment preferences. For example, M. A. Cohen, Rust, and Steen's recent (2006) study of public preferences for criminal justice spending priorities is particularly relevant here. Using a nationally representative sample, citizens were asked to rank order their public spending priorities according to their preferences for various alternatives (e.g., youth crime prevention, drug treatment for nonviolent offenders, more prisons, and so on). Cohen et al.'s study found that nearly 60 percent of the respondents favored focusing public spending on youth crime prevention and drug treatment. Alternatively, only 8.4 percent ranked "building more prisons" as the best option.[3] It is therefore clear that as policy makers continue to endorse the prison boom, their reliance on the justification of "giving the public what it wants" demonstrates, at best, ignorance and, at worst, willful contempt regarding the complexity of citizens' attitudes about punishment.

Public Support for Alternative Punishment Philosophies

As noted in Chapter 2, the idea that criminal offenders could be meaningfully changed through correctional rehabilitation strategies came under considerable ideological attack in the 1970s. As the get-tough movement gathered steam, the correctional philosophy of rehabilitation—which had been dominant since the Progressive Era of the late 1800s—took a backseat to the more hard-line concerns of retribution, deterrence, and incapacitation (Pratt et al. 1998). At the same time, policy makers eschewed rehabilitation strategies for offenders based on the assumption that the American public was fed up with such approaches. As a result, corrections policy makers once again felt at liberty to continue to increase the nation's prison population and to argue that the lock-'em-up strategy is the best way to control crime.

Such assumptions on the part of policy makers are problematic for two reasons. First, what is unique about the rehabilitative ideal is that it is the only correctional philosophy that obligates the state to be concerned about the offenders' needs (Cullen and Gilbert 1982). It is tempting—and perhaps not unreasonable—to take the position that offenders are not in prison for being model citizens, and therefore whatever harsh treatment they receive is deserved. Nevertheless, the reality is that the removal of the obligation of doing something positive for offenders has resulted in certain "collateral consequences"—namely, problems with successful reintegration into society (a point that will be elaborated in Chapter 6).

The second problem is that policy makers' assumptions about a generally punitive public once again miss the nuanced nature of how Americans feel about punishment. In particular, Americans are extremely utilitarian (Bellah et al. 1985; Garland 1990). As such, the broad trend in the empirical literature is that, yes, Americans want their correctional system to punish and to inflict some sort of pain (or, at minimum, some inconvenience) on offenders (Newman 1985). What Americans also want, however, is for the punishment side of corrections to coexist with the treatment/rehabilitative side. In short, Americans want it both ways in what has been dubbed a "hybrid" (Tonry 1998, 206), where retributive and utilitarian punishment rationales are intertwined. The real question, therefore, is not whether policy makers are correct to assume that American citizens have a punitive streak, but rather whether those same citizens are also willing to embrace rehabilitative strategies at the same time.

Public Support for Correctional Rehabilitation

Scholars and policy makers alike tend to highlight the apparent tension between the goals of punishment and those of rehabilitation. The American public, however, does not necessarily see it that way. To be sure, evidence that Americans want more from the correctional system than raw punitiveness is widespread (Applegate, Cullen, and Fisher 1997; Cullen, Cullen, and Wozniak 1988; Thomson and Ragona 1987; Warr and Stafford 1984). What is most compelling is the research indicating that, even after the pummeling the rehabilitative ideal took from Martinson (1974) and others, Americans still see rehabilitation as an important component of corrections.

On the one hand, given the general shift toward a more punitive philosophy for corrections, public support for rehabilitation as the "primary" goal for corrections has decreased in recent decades. In 1968, an estimated 73 percent of the American population indicated that rehabilitation should be the main goal of imprisonment, with only 7 percent choosing "punishment" and 12 percent choosing to "protect society" (Harris 1968). Three decades later, support for rehabilitation as the main goal for corrections had dropped to just over 26 percent, with nearly 60 percent of the respondents instead noting that the primary purpose of prisons should be to "punish and put away" lawbreakers (Maguire and Pastore 1997). Nowhere is this trend clearer than in the way the public feels about the rehabilitative potential of violent offenders. In a survey of Cincinnati residents, Sundt et al. (1998) found that only 13.8 percent of the respondents believed that rehabilitation would be "very helpful" or "helpful" for violent offenders, and a national study by Doble Research Associates (1995a) found that only 14.4 percent of the respondents believed that "most" violent offenders could be successfully rehabilitated.

Nevertheless, rehabilitation is still seen as an important part of the correctional setting by the American public. The same study by Sundt et al. (1998) revealed that nearly two-thirds of the sample indicated rehabilitation would be beneficial for nonviolent offenders, and the national study by Doble Research Associates (1995a) found that nearly half of those polled said correctional rehabilitation could be effective for "some" violent offenders. Furthermore, another national study by Flanagan (1996) found that the public strongly supports rehabilitation—as opposed to punishment or crime prevention/deterrence—for offenders once they are committed to prison.

In addition, researchers have noted how forcing survey respondents to choose a single goal for corrections may be hiding a key feature of how Americans feel about punishment—namely, that citizens want the correctional system to satisfy multiple goals at the same time (Warr 1994). For example, in a statewide survey of Ohio residents, Applegate et al. (1997) found that over 90 percent of the sample rated the goals of "protection and punishment" as important, yet 80 percent of these same respondents rated "rehabilitation" as equally important. These findings not only indicate that Americans' punishment preferences are multifaceted, but also that rehabilitation—a correctional philosophy capable of challenging the current overreliance on "prison-as-crime control"—still remains a viable goal in the mind of the American public.

Finally, the evidence that Americans still believe in the efficacy of rehabilitation is most compelling when examining how the public feels about the amenability of juvenile offenders to correctional treatment. Once guided by the notion of "child saving" and individualized treatment (Platt 1969), the juvenile justice system has undergone many of the same changes as the adult system, with a general shift toward greater punitiveness (Feld 1998). Yet despite the growing trend toward trying juvenile offenders as adults—a practice that has plenty of public support to back it up (Maguire and Pastore 1995; Roberts and Stalans 1997; Triplett 1996)—research indicates that citizens are even more supportive of rehabilitation for juveniles than for adult offenders (Cullen, Golden, and Cullen 1983; Moon et al. 2000), and Sundt et al. (1998) found that over 80 percent of their sample of Cincinnati residents reported that rehabilitation for juveniles would be helpful. In addition, Applegate et al.'s (1997, 247) Ohio study found that over 95 percent of the respondents agreed with the statement that "it is important to try to rehabilitate juveniles who have committed crimes and are now in the correctional system," and Doble Research Associates' (1995b) sample of Oregon residents found that over 90 percent of those surveyed concerning where they would prefer their corrections dollars to be spent chose to "rehabilitate juvenile offenders" over doing the same for adult offenders or to "punish juvenile offenders."

Public Support for Juvenile Justice

Consistent with the evidence presented above, public opinion also remains for a part of the criminal justice system that has always been more closely aligned with the philosophy and practice of correctional rehabilitation—the juvenile justice system. Emerging out of the early 20th-century Progressive Era, the system of juvenile justice rejected the adversarial and punishment-oriented approach of the adult criminal justice system in favor of a more informal method of intervening in the "best interests" of the child (Butts and Mears 2001). Academics have become concerned in the last couple of decades, however, as a number of states have slowly chipped away at the division between the juvenile and adult justice systems (Fagan and Zimring 2000; Kupchik 2003). Among these recent reforms are efforts to lower the upper age limit for the jurisdiction of the juvenile court, which helps to facilitate the transfer of youthful offenders to adult court (i.e., by lowering the age at which youths may be processed in adult criminal courts from what was typically 17–18 years old, down to 16 in some states; see Mears 2003; Snyder and Sickmund 2006).

Despite the political popularity of this movement, a recent statewide study of Florida residents by Mears et al. (2007) clearly shows that citizens still support the continued existence of a separate system of juvenile justice. In particular, their study revealed that roughly 80 percent of the state's respondents indicated they approved of keeping the juvenile justice system (with only a small minority favoring getting rid of it). While attitudes varied across individuals, support for juvenile justice remained strong even after controlling for a host of sociodemographic factors. Thus, political efforts to either eliminate the juvenile justice system (whether explicitly or implicitly by continuing to blur the line between the juvenile and adult systems), with its emphasis on the rehabilitation and reform of at-risk youths, are inconsistent with public views on the subject.

Public Support for Early Intervention Programs

Based in part on the empirical evidence that the American public is willing to suspend their "global" feelings of hostility when it comes to juvenile offenders, researchers have also tested the waters regarding the degree to which the public would support early intervention programs for at-risk juveniles. Rooted in the life course perspective in criminology (see, e.g., Laub and Sampson 2003; Moffitt 1993; Sampson and Laub 1993), which recognizes the impact of early childhood developmental processes on prosocial behavior in adulthood, early intervention programs target high-risk youths with the goal of preventing future offending (Farrington 1994).

Such programs have proven to be highly effective in reducing problem behaviors for the targeted children and adolescents (Farrington 1994; Howell and Hawkins 1998; Yoshikawa 1994), and the American public seems to be right "in step" with their support of such an approach. For example, Fairbank et al.'s (1997, 2) survey of California residents found that over 80 percent of the respondents noted their "biggest priority is to invest in ways to prevent kids from taking wrong turns and ending up in gangs, violence, or prison," while only 13 percent of the sample favored the option "to build more prisons and youth facilities and enforce stricter sentences to guarantee that the most violent juvenile offenders are kept off the street" (see also Cullen et al. 1998).

Summary

Moral panics are not uncommon in this country. Examples are plentiful of a single dramatic story—one that media organizations can descend upon—blowing reality all out of proportion. As a great example of this phenomenon, in 2001 a series of shark attacks off the East Coast garnered a ton of media attention. Americans were attacked from Florida up to Virginia Beach; surfers and swimmers were bitten, arms and feet were torn off, and there were even a couple of high-profile deaths.

Given this coverage, it would be easy to assume that shark attacks were at an all-time high in 2001. Confirmation would seem to come on September 4, 2001, when *Time* magazine published a special report called "The Summer of the Shark." But it wasn't so; instead, data from the International Shark Attack File at the Florida Museum of Natural History showed that both fatal and nonfatal shark attacks were actually down from 2000 (S. Miller 2003). It took the events of September 11, 2001, to kick killer sharks off the media rotation.

Despite such moral panics, and the often unreasonable policy responses they fuel, one of the hallmarks of any Western democracy is the input that citizens have over public policy decisions. Since lawmakers are not psychic, when it comes to certain policy choices they must inevitably rely on public opinion polls to provide a barometer concerning what their constituents do, or do not, want from them. At minimum, this tradition assumes that citizens are aware of the relative advantages and drawbacks of the various policy options at their representatives' disposal. On that front, although disagreements exist among scholars, the general consensus is that, when given adequate information, American citizens are better able to express their beliefs in ways that can be translated into public policies (Warr 1995). The problem is that, although citizens do, in fact, know "what they want" when it comes to punishment, much of the research addressing this question has failed to tap into the public's full range of preferences on the subject.

If so, it is likely that policy makers who continue to justify the increased growth of the incarcerated population under the auspices of "giving the public what it wants" are simply ignorant of the nuanced nature of public opinion about punishment. The alternative, of course (and an option that cannot be fully ruled out), is that policy makers "know better" yet continue to selectively use (or misuse) certain empirical findings concerning citizens' "global" attitudes as a means of gaining political capital. Either way, the result is still the same: enough misinformation about public opinion exists to provide policy makers with an excuse to avoid thinking about the purposes of punishment in ways other than beating the get-tough drum.

Yet perhaps this is too harsh an assessment of policy makers' decision processes. To their credit, public officials may have rational reasons—based on the incentives associated with their positions—to ignore constituents' complex views on punishment issues. For example, scholars who study legislative politics have long pointed out that policy proposals are more likely to survive the legislative process when they are written in a somewhat vague manner. The reason is that specificity on key points often leads to disagreements among other lawmakers who may have competing interests (despite, for example, their "global" support for the policy initiative; see R. E. Cohen 1992). Further, scholars who study both voting behavior and the media–politics link are well aware that acknowledging complexity and nuance can be political killers (Franz et al. 2007;

Graber 1993), where confessing to the existence of a "gray area" with regard to any policy proposal may risk earning one the title of "flip-flopper" (just ask former presidential hopeful John Kerry). It may therefore be a rational response on the part of policy makers to accept the results of global public opinion polls rather than risk getting themselves into political trouble by digging deeper into Americans' specific attitudes about crime and punishment.

In any event (whether my assessment of policy makers was fair or not), to the credit of the punitive-minded there is a mountain of empirical evidence indicating that, as Americans, not only do we like our punishment, but we seem to like it "Supersized." The problem, however, is that such "global" preferences are only part of the picture, and efforts to paint the American public as a thick-skulled, compassionless, bloodthirsty mob are decidedly disingenuous. As Cullen et al. (2000, 57) noted, when it comes to the normative purposes of punishment, "people's attitudes are complex and more ideologically diverse than they are commonly represented." Thus, there is no denying we like our punishment harsh, yet we are equally in favor of a correctional system that is charged with doing all that it can to change offenders for the better. Even further, Americans seem to place considerable faith in the efficacy of a correctional philosophy—rehabilitation—that is, to a large extent, at odds with the get-tough movement's reliance on crime control through incapacitation and deterrence. In the end, the broader theme of this chapter is that public support for "crime control through incarceration" is not nearly as rigid and unwavering as the talking-head proponents of such an approach would have us believe.

Notes

1. More examples certainly abound; the website www.dumbcrooks.com alone provides sufficient additional examples of this point.

2. Given the nature of public debate on the subject, including drug offenders in the category of nonviolent offenders may be debatable, especially since drug offenses are often correlated with violent offending (McGloin et al. 2007; C. J. Sullivan et al. 2006). Yet, consistent with both legal definitions and prior research (Austin and Irwin 2001), for the present purpose I am treating drug offending (e.g., possession) as a nonviolent offense.

3. It is also important to note that the typical respondent in M. A. Cohen et al.'s (2006) study would rather spend public resources on youth crime prevention and drug treatment than use those same dollars as a tax rebate back to him- or herself.

Five

Misinformation About Prisons and Crime Control

In late 2002, the Associated Press (AP) ran a brief story about that year's slight drop in crime (in fact, the rates of a number of offenses, including homicide, actually went up a bit that year, but why fret over the details?). Not to be accused of presenting facts without context, the AP writer buffered the story with quotes from two alleged "experts" in criminological research: an economist from Stanford University and a senior member of a research firm based in Chicago—both of whom contacted the AP directly. In a joint statement that probably caused old-school, get-tough advocates to beat their chests in triumph, these experts attributed the year's drop in crime to tougher sentencing laws and the nation's growing prison population (of course, these same causes were not cited as potential explanations for the increase in homicides the same year).

Since this was an AP news release, the story was picked up by newspapers from New York City to Kenosha, Wisconsin, and should have been the fatal blow to the arguments made by the touchy-feely liberals. Before the punitive crowd could let the champagne corks fly, however, there was just one teeny-tiny problem: it turned out that neither of the supposed "experts" even existed. The news release attracted numerous calls and e-mails from criminologists who had never heard of either scholar; there was no mention of such a name on the faculty list at Stanford, nor was there any information on the bogus research outfit in Chicago. Although a 5-minute Internet search would have revealed this information to any American citizen who can read at a sixth-grade level, the ruse was apparently convincing enough to somehow "dupe" the fact-checkers at the AP. In the end, these two yahoos posing as criminologists were able to slip by folks at the AP in their quest to get their fake message heard.

The goof on the part of the AP—as well as the rest of the nation—was short-lived. A couple of days later, the AP put out another news release that revealed the egg on their collective face. Not only did they admit that their expert sources were frauds, but they also noted that the individuals who pulled a fast one on them had called to gloat about it! Apparently, the pranksters contacted the AP again, expressing their delight, as well as their surprise, over how easily their statements (and faux credentials) were believed by the gullible AP staff.

Standards of journalistic integrity notwithstanding, this example points to a deeper problem in the realm of contemporary American crime control policy: the ubiquitous and unquestioned belief in the efficacy of prisons as a tool for crime control. To a certain extent, this belief is understandable given its intuitive appeal—that is, the prospect of doing time in prison strikes a note of fear among the general population, thus the threat of incarceration alone should serve as a valuable deterrent to crime. Furthermore, public concern over potential "incapacitation effects" of prisons—the crime control benefits associated with merely locking offenders up for a period of time—was virtually nonexistent prior to the prison construction boom of the 1980s (see, e.g., Zimring and Hawkins 1995), where before that time some level of crime reduction from an incapacitation effect was simply taken as a "given."

As such, calls from policy makers and the general public to increase the size of the incarcerated population as much as possible can still be heard. For example, in a 2003 op-ed piece to the *Lewiston Morning Tribune* in Lewiston, Idaho, one local resident raised a call to arms to fellow voters to expand Nez Perce County's jail space by imploring residents to "help protect yourself and those you love by building a jail that will protect us from being victimized, shot *or decapitated*" (emphasis added).

Such sentiments seem to vindicate the policy makers who place so much faith in the efficacy of incarceration as the preferred method for crime control. As the previous chapters indicate, however, the real world is often much more complex than the rhetorical world in which policy makers live. The purpose of this chapter, therefore, is to examine the empirical status of the research that scholars have produced in an effort to uncover whether prison expansion and related policy efforts *actually reduce crime.* To foreshadow the conclusions a bit, the evidence is, at best, pretty slim. The reasons behind such weak crime control effects for these get-tough strategies are also explored in this chapter—in particular, the comparative validity of the "bad implementation" argument (e.g., "we're just not tough enough") versus the "incomplete theory of offender decision making" as explanations for why locking up more and more offenders doesn't seem to do much to the crime rate.

The general conclusion reached in this chapter is that prisons give us, at most, precious little crime control in return for our public dollar. Some early challengers to the get-tough movement—those from the extreme "decarceration camp"—even went so far as to predict that a massive increase in incarceration rates over subsequent decades would result in a "zero" net reduction in crime (Nagel 1977). Such claims are also inconsistent with the empirical evidence; a nation that locks up over 2 million of its citizens can, and should, expect *some* drop in crime. The question is, how much of a drop can we expect, and how reliable is the information policy makers are using when they go about publicly addressing this question?

Prisons and Crime Control: The Empirical Evidence

By the beginning of the 1990s, the incarcerated population in the United States had increased by 600 percent since 1970 (Bureau of Justice Statistics 1998). What followed this incarceration boom was a decade that experienced a substantial decrease in crime rates—a trend that seemed to occur nationwide (Blumstein and Wallman 2000; Conklin 2003). Many policy makers saw this as an obvious indicator that the exponential increases in public resources devoted to building and maintaining the world's largest prison system were finally working. Since incarceration rates went up in the 1970s and 1980s, and crime went down in the 1990s—case closed!

The problem with this explanation is that there were a lot of things going on during the 1990s that also contributed to the drop in crime. Among these developments, researchers have pointed to the importance of improved economic conditions during that time, which may have eased the social strains associated with economic deprivation and provided greater access to legitimate employment (Grogger 2000; Pratt and Lowenkamp 2002); changes in the nature of inner-city drug markets that resulted in a severe drop in gang violence (Blumstein and Rosenfeld 1998; B. Johnson, Golub, and Dunlap 2000); and demographic changes that resulted in an aging—and therefore less crime-prone—population (Fox 2000; Gottfredson and Hirschi 1990; Sampson and Laub 1993). In order to isolate the independent contribution of an "incarceration effect" on crime, at minimum these other influences need to be controlled. Fortunately, a plethora of research has done just that.

Estimating the Effects of Prison Expansion on Crime Rates

The logic behind some sort of "incarceration effect" on the crime rate is simple: To begin with, prisons by their nature should have some ability to incapacitate. That is, at minimum, offenders will be unable to victimize anyone (with the exception of other inmates, of course) during their stay behind bars (Greenberg 1975). What's more attractive for incarceration advocates, however, is the potential for prisons in general—and prison expansion in particular—to exert a widespread deterrent effect on the would-be offender population.

Simply put, the deterrence perspective assumes that offenders exercise rational judgment and are reasonably aware of the potential costs associated with various criminal acts (Pratt et al. 2006; see also Becker 1968). This assumption translates generally into the proposition that crime rates in any given region can be curbed by the crime control activities of the criminal justice system (i.e., by increasing the potential "costs" and probable "risks" for criminal behavior). Such activities can come in the form of more rigorous police practices (e.g., crackdowns, increasing clearance rates, increasing police size; see Greenberg, Kessler, and Logan 1979; Logan 1975; Marvell and Moody 1996; Mazerolle, Kadleck, and Roehl 1998; Sampson and Cohen 1988; J. Q. Wilson and Boland 1978), the more frequent use of the death penalty (Cochran, Chamlin, and Seth 1994; Peterson and Bailey 1991), and increasing the penalties for certain offenses (McDowall, Loftin, and Wiersema 1992). The central empirical claim for deterrence advocates, therefore, is that these types of public efforts "matter" and they should, independent of other social processes, have an appreciable effect on rates of crime.[1]

Deterrence theory, of course, is not new. Cesare Beccaria and Jeremy Bentham both contributed to early versions of the rational choice model in the late 1700s. Bentham's notion of the "hedonic calculus," where humans were assumed to have free will and to respond to the certainty, swiftness, and severity of punishments, was particularly influential in the redevelopment of legal structures throughout Western Europe (Lilly et al. 2007). For example, nations began to restrict the severity of legally proscribed punishments so that they would not extend beyond what was necessary (at least in theory) for the prevention and deterrence of specific offenses (e.g., it was no longer viewed as "rational" that the penalties for, say, murder and pick-pocketing be the same—public hanging; see R. Johnson 1990). This new view of punishment also played a significant role in the French Revolution and the development of the United States Constitution (Rothman 1971).

Deterrence theory in its more contemporary form is really no more complex than it was in its original version (see, e.g., Becker 1968); it still relies heavily on the central assumption that criminal behavior can be controlled through formal penalties, and it still emphasizes the role that purposive choice plays in criminal behavior (Cornish and Clarke 1986). On the one hand, the resurgence of the rational choice model in criminology has been a welcome shot in the arm for academics: no longer would offenders merely be viewed as "empty vessels" waiting to be filled up with the social and psychological risk factors that would propel them to commit crime (Lilly et al. 2007, 277). Viewing offenders instead as conscious decision makers capable of purposive action has undoubtedly moved our understanding of criminal behavior forward in important ways (e.g., see the discussion in Pratt et al. 2006). Yet on the other hand, Lilly et al. (2007) note that

> The danger in rational choice theory [is] that offenders will be treated as though they [are] *only decision makers*. When this occurs, the context that affects why they come to the point of breaking the law is ignored, and commentators begin to recommend harsh criminal justice policies that ignore the social context and focus only on making crime a costly decision. (p. 277, emphasis in the original)

Another key problem with deterrence theory, and one that is more relevant to the discussion of prisons-as-crime-control contained in this chapter, is that of separating potential deterrent effects of prison (or at least the threat of prison) from the other factors that control our behavior (e.g., other forms of informal social control at the individual level, such as self-control and social bonds, and at the community level, such as concentrated disadvantage and collective efficacy). Nevertheless, what prisons present is the potential combination of deterrence and incapacitation. Thus, what is most relevant for this discussion is the body of studies that have examined the potential deterrent and incapacitative qualities of prisons.

Accordingly, much of the contemporary political rhetoric concerning the effect that increasing prison populations has exerted on crime rates has relied on the use of "bivariate" relationships. What this means is that increases in the incarcerated population are tracked against changes in crime rates over time (perhaps with the help of visual aids to make the point even more obvious), with attention explicitly focused only on those two variables—a practice seen quite frequently in the *New York Times* coverage of crime rates throughout the 1990s (Conklin 2003). There are two problems with this methodological approach. First, as stated above, multiple factors contribute to the crime problem in the United States, where scholars have systematically revealed the importance of individual factors such as internal control capabilities (e.g., impulsivity and the lack of self-control; see Pratt and Cullen 2000); systems of informal social control acting upon individuals (e.g., parental controls, supervision and control maintained by social institutions such as schools and communities; see Pratt, Turner, and Piquero 2004; Turner, Piquero, and Pratt 2005); and antisocial attitudes (Andrews and Bonta 1998) to macro-level factors including economic deprivation, family disruption, and low levels of community social capital (Pratt and Cullen 2005). Thus, thinking about crime requires a "multivariate" (as opposed to a bivariate) approach—a point that is elaborated more fully later in this chapter. Should these factors be ignored in the explanation of crime rates over time, the "incarceration effect" is likely to be overstated (Nagin 1978, 1998a).

The second problem, which is a bit more technical, is what researchers refer to as the "endogeneity problem" (Nagin 1998b). Put simply, when assessing the effect of prisons on crime rates, it must also be noted that increases in crime are likely to result in increases in the prison population. This makes sense because rising crime rates are likely to be met with a proportional response from criminal justice agencies that should, over time, result in an increase in prison populations. This "reciprocal effect" of crime on prison populations must therefore be taken into account statistically in order to estimate the effect of prisons on crime (i.e., by first estimating the effect of crime on prisons).

So what do the studies that have used multivariate models and have taken into account the endogeneity problem show with regard to the effect of prison expansion on crime rates? The estimates differ a bit, but they all follow the same broad trend: strategies that entail greater use of incarceration result in, at best, a modest reduction in crime yet also result in a substantial increase in prison population. In particular, Visher (1987) noted that a 1 percent reduction in crime would require a 10 to 20 percent increase in the prison population (see also Blumstein et al. 1986; cf. Spelman 1994)—an effect that has remained stable in subsequent studies (Spelman 2000). At our current levels, this would mean between 220,000 and 440,000 additional inmates, at a cost of around $25,000 per inmate per year, for a total price tag of between $5.5 billion and $11 billion to get that 1 percent reduction in crime. Put differently, each time we double our prison population—something we've done multiple times in recent decades—we get a drop in crime of between 5 and 10 percent in return.

Things look even bleaker when you compare the extent to which expansions in incarceration predict crime rates relative to other social and economic factors. For example, Pratt and Cullen's (2005) meta-analysis of over 200 studies on the predictors of crime rates found that the overall "effect size" (interpreted as the strength of the relationship) of incarceration variables that have been adjusted for endogeneity and crime rates was among the weakest of the 31 different predictors assessed. The strongest predictors of crime rates were found to be variables that tapped into "concentrated disadvantage," which is the intersection of economic deprivation and family disruption concentrated within particular racial groups in society (see also Sampson, Raudenbush, and Earls 1997; Sampson and Wilson 1995; W. J. Wilson 1987); long-term chronic unemployment (see also Land, Cantor, and Russell 1995); and stingy social policies that undermine levels of social support for citizens (see also Cullen 1994; DeFronzo 1996, 1997; Pratt and Godsey 2002, 2003).

The unmistakable conclusion from this collection of studies is that policy makers' claims of massive reductions in crime that can be attributed to the expansion of the prison population are patently false. Yet this is not to say that our "prison experiment" has yielded no reduction in crime rates. Even the meager percentage of reduction in crime that prisons give us is no small matter in a country that experiences far more violent crime than any other Western nation. The impact of prisons on crime, however, which perhaps more than any other single factor has enabled our dependence on incarceration, is quite weak when considered in light of the dollars that state and federal corrections budgets absorb that could be spent addressing the underlying social factors more strongly related to crime rates.

Why the Weak Effects?

It is clear that policy makers who continue to justify prison expansion—or even the maintenance of our current levels of incarceration—because of its crime control merits can only do so in the face of a mountain of solid empirical evidence that points to the limited role of incarceration in controlling crime. In fact, much of policy makers' rhetoric justifying the aggressive use of incarceration to enhance public safety isn't rooted in empirical evidence at all. It is instead typically based on appeals to the intuitive nature of our fear of being subjected to harsh sanctions. Such appeals inevitably beg the question of why "prison effects" on crime aren't as large as we've been led to believe.

Faulty Implementation of the Get-Tough Philosophy

One explanation favored by deterrence/incapacitation advocates is that, despite our efforts to "get tough" over the last few decades, we still need to "get tougher." In essence, this argument assumes that we are on the right track "in spirit" but that we just aren't doing a good enough job of implementing the get-tough philosophy. Putting this concretely, despite our mammoth prison system, some scholars contend that we've only been "inching up" our criminal sanctions in recent years (J. Q. Wilson 1996, 296), while others have recently compared the American criminal justice system to a "revolving door of leniency" (Delisi 2005, 145). Citing estimates that offenders—even those convicted of violent crimes—rarely serve their full sentences, policy makers' efforts to step up punishments even more are bolstered by academics' claims that

> Today and every day the "justice" system permits known, convicted, violent repeat criminals, adult and juvenile to get away with murder and mayhem on the streets. Criminals who have repeatedly violated the life, liberty, and property of others are routinely set free to do it all over again. (Bennett et al. 1996)

In the spirit of misinformation, policy makers also have at their disposal government reports that can be creatively interpreted to indicate that murderers can expect to serve an average of 1.8 years in prison, rapists can expect 60 days, and robbers around 23 days (Langan and

Graziadei 1995; Langan, Perkins, and Chaiken 1995). These estimates are derived by dividing the amount of prison time spent by offenders nationwide by the number of crimes of these types that are committed each year.

The problem, however, is that such evidence fails to take into account the fact that many offenses—even violent crimes—rarely make it to the sentencing phase of the criminal justice system (Bureau of Justice Statistics 1999). Moreover, those that do typically do not result in a prison sentence, and for good reasons. For example, many crimes fail to result in an arrest; of those that do, nearly a third are committed by juvenile offenders who may be punished, yet rarely with a sentence of prison time in an adult facility. Other defendants have their cases dismissed or are found not guilty at trial (S. Walker 2001). The fact that this "funneling" takes place is neither unfair nor overly lenient; it is merely the result of the reasonable disposition of cases in the criminal justice system.

Once this is taken into account, we see that serious crimes that are reported to the police, that result in an arrest and conviction (a small fraction of all offenses by any estimation)—in other words, those that eventually make it to the sentencing stage—have always been dealt with harshly in this country. For example, nearly 90 percent of offenders convicted of felony robbery end up being incarcerated; roughly the same figure (88 percent) goes for those convicted of rape (Langan and Brown 1997). Furthermore, when limiting the analysis to those convicted and sentenced, we find that murderers spend an average of around 10 years in prison (not 1.8), that rapists spend an average of nearly 7 years (not 60 days), and robbers over 4 years (not 23 days) in prison—sentences that far exceed those of other Western nations (W. Young and Brown 1993). In the end, therefore, the claim that the reason "incarceration effects" on crime aren't as large as promised is that we've failed to fully implement the get-tough model falls flat when misinformation about American punitiveness—what Currie (1998, 38) calls the "myth of leniency"—is exposed.

Incapacitation and the Age-Crime Curve

One alternative explanation for the relatively weak estimates of the incapacitation effect has to do with an amazingly consistent pattern of criminal offending over the life course: the "aging out effect." Although scholars disagree about the causal mechanisms at work (see, e.g., Gottfredson and Hirschi 1990; Laub and Sampson 2003; Moffitt 1993; Sampson and Laub 1993), virtually every longitudinal data set available shows the same trend over time, where individuals' participation in criminal activity peaks for a short period of time from the late teens to the early 20s and begins a steady downward decline after that (see, e.g., Blumstein et al. 1986; J. Cohen 1986; Farrington 1986, 1989; Nagin and Land 1993; Piquero et al. 2003; Piquero, Brame, and Lynam 2004).

Early attempts at estimating incapacitation effects, however, failed to incorporate this well-known criminological phenomenon. For example, Zedlewski's (1987) ringing endorsement of the benefits of an incapacitation strategy concluded that locking up offenders—who he estimated commit on average 187 crimes per year—for an extended period of time should cut crime dramatically. Suspicious of such estimates, Zimring and Hawkins' (1988) reassessment of the data revealed that, if correct, given the amount of prison expansion that occurred during the prior decade, Zedlewski's estimates of incapacitation effects predicted that the United States should have been completely crime free by 1986. That obviously didn't happen.

Part of Zedlewski's problem can be traced to the way incarceration has been used in recent years, with a greater proportion of prison beds being filled with drug offenders—a crime that has an extremely high "replacement effect," where the removal of one drug user from a community is generally met with another to take that person's place (Mauer 1999). Even so, the greater methodological problem that such studies suffer from is that they fail to recognize individual-level declines in criminal activity over time (see also DiIulio and Piehl 1991). As a result, incapacitation estimates that assume an individual's rate of offending at, say, 17 years of age will continue for the next 20 years will always be artificially inflated. Studies that instead take this pattern into account all point to a more modest estimate of the effect of prison expansion on crime rates (Visher 1987).

The Limits of Fear-Based Crime Control Policy

One final, and perhaps most empirically viable, alternative explanation for why the incapacitation bang for the prison buck tends to be rather paltry points to the limited role that the fear of formal sanctioning plays in controlling our behavior. Put differently, the problem with emphasizing the use of incarceration—especially the *threat* of incarceration—to control crime may have less to do with debates concerning whether or not we've properly implemented a deterrence-theory model for criminal behavior. The problem may simply be with deterrence theory itself.

Rooted in the classical school of criminology and its rational choice view of human behavior (see Beccaria 1764/1963), deterrence theory possesses two features that increase its appeal to policy makers. First, the deterrence approach offers an easily understood, straightforward *explanation of crime:* individuals choose to go into crime when it "pays"—that is, when the benefits outweigh the costs. People may not always be perfectly rational, but they are reasonably aware of the potential costs and benefits associated with criminal acts. When faced with the prospect that wayward behavior will elicit punishment, they are likely to "think twice" and be "deterred" from choosing this course of action.

Second, the deterrence approach offers an easily understood, straightforward *solution to crime:* the choice of crime can be made less attractive by implementing policies that heighten the costs of illegal conduct—that is, laws and penalties that ensure that criminal participation "does not pay" (Nagin 1998a). It seems only a matter of common sense that raising the costs or likely risks of crime should involve the criminal justice system, the state's instrument for detecting the criminally wayward and inflicting punishment on them.

The problem for deterrence disciples is the body of empirical studies that has tested the proposition that our fear of formal sanctioning should influence our likelihood of engaging in criminal behavior. For example, Pratt et al.'s (2006) meta-analysis of 40 studies on perceptual deterrence—those that assessed individuals' perceptions of the certainty and severity of punishment—found that these deterrence-based predictors were, at best, only weakly associated with criminal behavior (see also Paternoster 1987). Furthermore, the effect sizes of the deterrence variables are substantially reduced—often to zero—in multivariate models. This trend is particularly evident for the effect size estimates produced by statistical models that control for peer effects, antisocial attitudes, or levels of self-control (i.e., other well-known risk factors for criminal behavior). This finding points to the fact that support for the deterrence perspective is most likely to be found in studies that are methodologically the weakest of the bunch. Taken one step further, the clear drop in predictive power of the deterrence variables in this context suggests that empirical support for the effect of formal sanctions on individuals' criminal behavior—the linchpin of deterrence theory—is most likely an artifact of the failure to control for other "known" predictors of crime and deviance.

The weak predictive strength of deterrence variables may also explain why a host of other punitive crime control policies (e.g., mandatory minimum sentences) and correctional programs that rely on punishment threats (e.g., boot camps, intensive supervision, probation/parole) are limited in their capacity to effect long-term behavioral change among offenders (see, e.g., Cullen et al. 2002; Cullen et al. 1996; Petersilia and Turner 1993). A number of meta-analyses of the correctional treatment literature have even found that correctional programs that target offenders' fear of enhanced punishments may actually do more harm than good—especially among low-risk offenders (Andrews et al. 1990; Lipsey 1992; see also Pratt 2002).[2] Instead, successful programs tend to target factors that are not specified by deterrence theory, such as cognitive-behavioral programs that focus on changing antisocial attitudes (see Gensheimer et al. 1986; Gottschalk et al. 1987; Izzo and Ross 1990; Losel and Koferl 1989; Mayer et al. 1986; Wells-Parker and Bangert-Drowns 1991).

Rethinking Offender Decision Making

Contrary to get-tough advocates' assumptions concerning the effect of prisons on the would-be offenders' psyches, individuals' motivations to engage in criminal behavior are complex. Simple explanations—as comforting and useful as they may be for those with political aspirations—represent a fundamental misunderstanding of why people break the law. An important first step in the process of clearing up the misinformation about prisons and crime control requires an understanding of the factors that actually do matter when thinking about the causes of crime.

First and foremost, we need to get comfortable with the fact that multiple factors enter into an individual's behavioral choices in any given situation. Some of these factors have to do with the situation itself. For example, independent of whether someone believes he or she will get caught, some criminal opportunities are easier than others (e.g., items that can be stolen and easily concealed, potential robbery or assault victims that may be physically less able to fight back). Accordingly, some scholars have argued that such factors—referred to as "target attractiveness"—are so powerful that it takes very little "criminal motivation" for an individual to engage in crime (Clarke 1995; Clarke and Cornish 2001; L. E. Cohen and Felson 1979; Cornish and Clarke 1986; Felson 2002; Felson and Cohen 1980).

Others, however, note that individuals' perceptions of the attractiveness of criminal opportunities are shaped by a host of additional factors. In other words, not everyone who enters into a particular situation sees a criminal opportunity, so what makes those who take advantage of those opportunities different from those who don't? Research addressing this question has showed that one's level of self-control plays an important role in this decision process (Nagin and Pogarsky 2003; Piquero and Tibbetts 1996). In particular, those with low impulse control are less able to control their immediate urges, are less likely to be able to effectively evaluate the consequences of their actions, and are less likely to think that they'll get caught should they engage in criminal behavior (Pratt and Cullen 2000; see also McGloin and Pratt 2003; Pratt et al. 2006).

Self-control, in turn, comes from somewhere; research has indicated that biological factors (e.g., neuropsychological deficits, ADHD; see McGloin, Pratt, and Maahs 2004; Pratt et al. 2002; Unnever, Cullen, and Pratt 2003; J. P. Wright and Beaver 2005) can influence levels of self-control in children (see also McGloin, Pratt, and Piquero, 2006; Pratt et al. 2006). In addition, research has indicated the importance of effective parenting for the development of kids' self-control—parents need to consistently monitor their child's behavior and establish proper reinforcement contingencies to teach the child how to avoid succumbing to the temptation and immediate gratification that criminal/deviant acts can provide (Hay 2001; Perrone et al. 2004). Recent studies have even pointed to the importance of school socialization and its role in the development of self-control (Turner et al. 2005; see also the review in Pratt 2008).

The picture gets even more complex when examining the research that addresses how these individual-level risk factors are embedded within a larger social context. For example, studies have shown that parental efficacy is not only a strong risk factor for criminal behavior in offspring, but it is also significantly affected by adverse neighborhood conditions, such as economic deprivation and general disorder (Pratt et al. 2004). Conditions of neighborhood-level disorganization, in turn, are strongly related to higher rates of crime and victimization (Lowenkamp, Cullen, and Pratt 2003). Taking a further step back, research has indicated that such neighborhood problems are generally the result of larger social and economic forces, such as overall inequality and varying levels of social support across macro-social units (Pratt and Cullen 2005; Pratt and Godsey 2003). Thus, the bottom line is that we can't continue to cling to the oversimplified notion that a strict reliance on "scaring" would-be offenders—or simply holding them for a while before turning them loose—is the best way to achieve large reductions in crime.

Summary

The notion that mass incarceration is the most effective way to control crime appears to be a matter of unquestioned faith among American policy makers. As intuitive as this assumption is, it is inconsistent with the empirical evidence generated by over 200 studies of the predictors of crime rates (Pratt and Cullen 2005), 40 studies of the perceptions of formal sanctions on criminal behavior (Pratt et al. 2006), and over 400 studies of the effects of get-tough– versus nondeterrence-based correctional interventions (Lipsey 1992). To the extent that the construction of responsible "evidence-based" correctional policies is desirable, the existing evidence on the subject is clear: fear of criminal justice sanctions (including the threat of incarceration) is merely one factor—and a relatively weak one at that—influencing offender decision making.

Even scholars who champion (and end up overstating) the effect of prisons on crime suffer from a form of intellectual schizophrenia when thinking about the causes of crime. For example, Levitt and Dubner (2005) contend that high crime rates are caused by our "lenient criminal justice system" (p. 122). Accordingly, criminologists who doubt this proposition and instead focus on the social and individual/pathological sources of criminal behavior are simply accused of clinging to "figments of someone's imagination, self-interest, or wishful thinking" (p. 121). Others, like DiIulio (1995, 15), take this sentiment a step further and contend that "Apparently, it takes a Ph.D. in criminology to doubt that keeping dangerous criminals incarcerated cuts crime."

Despite the "leniency causes crime" thesis, however, Levitt and Dubner (2005, 124) go on to acknowledge that a reliance on prisons fails "to address the root causes of crime, which are diverse and complex." The last time I checked, the perception of "leniency" on the part of the criminal justice system—the key "cause" of crime according to Levitt and Dubner's own argument—is neither diverse nor complex. And therein lies the attractiveness of thinking about crime according to these terms: what makes the deterrence argument so seductive for policy makers is that it provides them with a simple explanation of the crime problem—as one that can be "cured" through prison expansion without having to address the more complex issues of the criminogenic effects of structured inequalities and other social and psychological sources of criminal behavior.

Even John DiIulio (1999) has recently claimed that "two million prisoners are enough" and that our current rate of prison expansion—one that he'd advocated just a few years ago (DiIulio 1994)—"is a portrait in the law of rapidly diminishing returns." He has thus abandoned his one-note "lock 'em up" tune and is now trumpeting the message of "zero prison growth." It seems that even the prison boom's biggest academic cheerleader has put down the pom-poms and has recognized the limits of crime control through incarceration.

In the end, the continued reliance on incarceration to control citizens' behavior can only be justified on the basis of misinformation about the efficacy of prisons as a tool for crime reduction. Again, this is not to say that the net effect of incarceration strategies on crime is zero; rather, the collective findings from the empirical research indicate that the effect is relatively small given the amount of resources we devote to it. Furthermore, the wisdom of expanded imprisonment must be weighed against its costs financially as well as its questionable impact on the social vitality of inner cities. On that note, a number of scholars have conducted studies indicating that a high rate of incarceration may *indirectly increase* crime rates through its effect on both family disruption and the potential economic deprivation brought on by the loss of an additional (or perhaps the only) income in a household (Pratt and Cullen 2005; see also Lynch and Sabol 2000; Rose and Clear 1998; Tonry 1995; W. J. Wilson 1987, 1996). This potential threat is heightened given the disproportionately high incarceration rates among members of racial/ethnic minority groups (Donziger 1996). Put simply, our love affair with incarceration has spawned a host of social consequences that may, in the long term, be just as harmful as the crime problem itself—an issue that is addressed in the next chapter.

Notes

1. It must be noted that, empirically, the claims of success for proponents of policies such as these are just that—claims. Little in the way of social scientific support can be marshaled to indicate that these types of criminal justice approaches are capable of meaningfully influencing crime rates (Pratt and Cullen 2005).

2. Scholars disagree as to why this effect is found among lower-risk offenders. It is most likely due to a combination of the exposure of lower-risk offenders to a population of more serious offenders and to the collateral consequences of experiencing harsh penalties (e.g., the disruption of social bonds and the limited services for reintegration)—topics to be discussed in depth in Chapter 6.

PART III

In Northern Michigan, Lake County has an interesting history with the African American community. In the early 1900s, the property around Idlewild Lake was developed into a resort community for vacationing blacks (Histed 2003; L. Walker and Wilson 2002). The resort's developers (two white brothers) recognized the market for such a community since African Americans were systematically excluded from white establishments at the time. In this new "Black Eden," the guest list included middle-class and well-to-do African Americans from Chicago, Cleveland, Detroit, and Indianapolis, not to mention entertainment figures such as Louis Armstrong, Count Basie, and Cab Calloway (Walker and Wilson, p. 17). The Idlewild community increased steadily in the next few decades, with a year-round population that continued to grow well into the 1960s. Even James Brown and Bill Cosby could be spotted as guests during this time.

The civil rights movement of the 1960s, however, changed Lake County in fundamentally important ways. With the advent of legally enforced desegregation, no longer would African Americans be limited to black-only establishments in their performance, entertainment, or vacationing options. Instead, social institutions (including resort venues) that were formerly off-limits to African Americans were now open. The impact on Idlewild was "devastating" (Histed 2003, 66). Interest in the area dissipated, businesses closed, buildings were demolished, and hotels and nightclubs sat empty. The result was that a once thriving community was plunged into economic deprivation.

Given the chronic unemployment rate that plagued Lake County up through the 1990s, the region became an attractive location for Michigan's Republican governor to locate a new juvenile prison. So in 1994, then-governor Engler—who was vying for reelection by pushing a get-tough crime control agenda—contracted with a private firm (Wackenhut

Corporation) to build and manage a juvenile facility, which he referred to publicly as both his "baby" and as Michigan's "punk prison" (Histed 2003, 40). Thus was the revival of the Idlewild region of Lake County, Michigan: where at one time buses carried loads of affluent African Americans ready to get away from it all at a resort community, those same buses now carry loads of economically deprived and (primarily) African American youths who are being carted away from the rest of society.

This is but one example of social transformation, yet it clearly demonstrates how getting tough through incarceration has consequences for our society, our communities, and our social institutions. Consistent with this theme, this section of the book is focused on the costs and consequences of our efforts at formal social control (mass incarceration). By "costs," however, I am not referring to the raw economics of the prison industry—the public expenditures associated with prison expansion are obvious enough. Of course, a portion of the $50 billion spent each year on prisons could be devoted elsewhere. Instead, the chapters in this section define "costs" more broadly to include not only direct economic impacts (e.g., on national levels of income inequality, profits made from prison privatization), but also the human costs of our addiction to incarceration (e.g., its effect on offender reintegration and the toll taken on inner-city communities).

Six

The Social Costs of Incarceration

In the late 19th century, the state of Washington developed a plan to create two public institutions, both of which were deemed necessary in the political context of the time: a state penitentiary and a land grant state college. Rather than locate either institution in the budding metropolis of Seattle or its outlying areas, the state legislature instead proposed placing both in the comparatively rural east side of the state. As the luck of the draw would have it, the community of Walla Walla was presented with the first pick—they could choose to have either the penitentiary or the college in their midst, either of which would provide a substantial public investment in their tiny little burg. Based on public perceptions of what would keep the community economically more viable in the long run, Walla Walla chose the penitentiary. As a default, the State College of Washington (now Washington State University) went to the neighboring farming hamlet of Pullman.

In the years that followed, the two communities could not have become more different. Pullman has flourished. It has enjoyed the economic benefits of the presence of a large research university, a well-educated population of full-time residents, nearly 20,000 spend-happy (if a bit rowdy) students, and a large influx of statewide dollars during the Division I, Washington State Cougars football season. Walla Walla, on the other hand, has been engaged in a constant struggle to shed the identity of being a "prison town." Despite a strong agricultural tradition in the region, famous onions, Whitman College, and a current cultural renaissance associated with its new identity as wine country, Walla Walla has fought to lose the stigma of merely being a prison town. And unlike Pullman, economic growth in Walla Walla has been slower to come in the last century, a trend that is fairly pervasive among communities where a prison is—or is at least perceived to be—the dominant industry (Hooks et al. 2004).

This is but one example, yet it reflects the broader struggle that policy makers routinely go through regarding how to distribute resources in a way that is consistent with the incentives they feel are upon them. In the United States—especially recently—those decisions have followed the general trend of cannibalizing the budgets of agencies charged with the task of social support and service (e.g., education, health care) to feed those of social control (e.g., prisons). In short, political decisions have consequences, particularly when they are tied to perceptions regarding what constitutes a good long-term public investment.

Accordingly, up until this point, the discussion in this book has focused on incarceration as an outcome of, at least in part, the presence and use of misinformation concerning a number of purported justifications for prison expansion. It is equally important, however, to highlight how our addiction to incarceration has itself contributed to a number of other social problems in the United States. That is the focus of this chapter.

In particular, the following sections detail the social costs of incarceration in the form of harm our addiction to incarceration has done to (1) offenders themselves in terms of the heightened risk of personal victimization while serving a prison sentence, and the barriers that incarceration poses for successful offender reintegration into society; (2) communities, in terms of how recent trends in the spatial distribution of the neighborhoods from which our primary incarcerated population is drawn have contributed to the further breakdown of inner-city communities, as well as how incarceration has reinforced and exacerbated existing racial inequalities; and (3) our social institutions, in terms of how incarceration has replaced other social services (e.g., public and mental health care) that were previously charged with the tasks of dealing with public problems, and how our obsession with providing additional prison space has resulted in the state's abdication of punishment to the private sphere and what the profit motive has done (and is continuing to do) to the practice of punishment.

Consequences of Incarceration for Offenders

Experiences in prison matter for those who are incarcerated. It is easy for both American citizens and public policy makers to forget about inmates once they are locked away and out of our sight. But offenders continue to gather life experience—and much of it is negative—during their stay in prison. Not surprisingly, many of these prison experiences are directly harmful to their success on the outside. At minimum, as offenders become more adjusted to prison life by adopting elements of the inmate code (e.g., the quick display of aggression, disrespect for institutional authority; see Sykes 1958), the prosocial values and attitudes that they need in order to be successful upon release will inevitably atrophy. Even more harmful is the heightened risk of personal victimization inside of prison (Wooldredge 1998). Victimization has severe psychological and emotional consequences for all victims of crime (Jones and Pratt, forthcoming), and inmates are no different. In short, the experience of incarceration has negative consequences for the offenders themselves.

Heightened Risk of Personal Victimization Within Prison

Prisons are not safe places. The deteriorating conditions of many facilities, coupled with the fact that the stream of incoming inmates has outmatched states' ability to "keep up" by constructing new prison space (Austin and Irwin 2001; Colson 1989; Mauer 1999; Pratt and Maahs 1999), have resulted in the diminished ability of correctional administrators to maintain order within prisons (Colvin 1992). As a result, concerns over rising levels of institutional violence have garnered the attention of correctional practitioners and policy makers alike (Eichenthal and Jacobs 1991).

Accordingly, the issue of prison violence and victimization has been the subject of considerable academic attention. The broad trend in this body of research indicates that prison violence, whether at the individual or institutional level, is the consequence of a host of complex factors. Some of these factors are considered "environmental," such as the level of crowding, quality of administrative control, and the security designation of the facility (Anson and Hancock 1992; Gaes and McGuire 1985; McCain, Cox, and Paulus 1980; Megargee 1976; Reisig 2002; Useem and Reisig 1999), while other factors are more "situational" (Wooldredge

1998), or individual-specific (Bowker 1980; Harer and Steffensmeier 1996; Wooldredge 1994). More recent work on the subject, using more sophisticated, multilevel statistical modeling techniques, has revealed that certain individual and institutional-level factors (such as the age of the inmate and the degree to which a facility is overcrowded) significantly interact with one another to increase the likelihood that an inmate will engage in misbehavior and victimize other inmates (Wooldredge, Griffin, and Pratt 2001; see also Camp et al. 2003).

Scholars have also focused their attention on more particular types of criminal victimization inside prisons—for example, sexual victimization among inmates (Jones and Pratt, forthcoming; see also Dumond 2000). Given rape's established place in the mythology of prison life, few are surprised by the assertion that inmates may be sexually victimized in prison (Mariner 2001). Accordingly, there is a general consensus among correctional administrators and practitioners that sexual victimization alters the social climate of the prison, contributes to aggregate levels of institutional violence, and results in physical and psychological trauma on the part of victims (Nacci and Kane 1983; N. E. Smith and Batiuk 1989; Struckman-Johnson et al. 1996).

Overall, what we do know is that for victims of violence in prison, the effects can be quite pervasive and damaging. For example, some scholars have focused on the physical effects of victimization (Mariner 2001), including injuries from a violent physical attack as well as the increased risk for acquiring a sexually transmitted disease or infection from sexual assaults (Kunselman et al. 2002). Others have studied the psychological effects of victimization in prison, such as post-traumatic stress disorder, stress response syndrome, and rape trauma syndrome (Dumond 2003; Knowles 1999; Kupers 1996; Mariner 2001; McCorkle 1993), all of which may affect the victim's behavioral and cognitive functioning (Dumond 2000; Lockwood 1980; Mariner 2001). Still others have examined the negative social costs associated with victimization in prison. Specifically, inmates who have been victimized may endure secondary effects in the form of lifestyle changes, disruption in social relations, changes in racial attitudes, and the loss of social status in exchange for stigmatization (Lockwood 1980; Mariner 2001). Furthermore, all of these problems are potentially exacerbated since victims tend to be at an increased risk for repeat victimization after being "marked" (Mariner 2001). In the end, given the size of the U.S. prison population, violent victimization has the potential to affect countless individuals. While victims of violence in prison suffer dramatically, society is faced with a population of (primarily) men who have been physically, psychologically, and socially harmed. Furthermore, the communities into which these inmates are released are left to grapple with some of the most devastating consequences of sexual violence, such as HIV and AIDS (Gido 2002).

Nevertheless, violence in prison has largely remained "America's most ignored crime problem" (Dumond 2003, 354). Correctional institutions have been criticized for turning a blind eye to such problems and for approaching criminal behavior inside of prisons with ignorance and indifference (Hensley, Tewksbury, and Castle 2003; C. D. Mann and Cronan 2001). In addition, American society may be guilty of accepting prison violence as a part of prison life, largely because of the belief that inmates are "undeserving" of protection, and that victimization in prison is a natural "consequence" of having violated society's norms and mores (Hassine 1999; Kury and Smartt 2002; Scacco 1984). Regardless of such perceptions and beliefs, the reality is that violence in prison is a crime that not only affects inmates, but also destabilizes institutional security and has the potential to compromise the physical health of communities into which these inmates are released—the topic to be covered in the following section.

Incarceration as a Barrier to Successful Offender Reintegration

As indicated in Figure 6.1, each year roughly 600,000 inmates will be released into various communities across the United States, primarily via the mechanism of parole release (Bureau of Justice Statistics 2007b; see also Austin and Irwin 2001). Given this large group of lawbreakers returning to society, it is not surprising that public attention will get focused on how well they do upon release. Such attention is warranted since, on the whole, recidivism rates for released inmates are fairly high: more than 60 percent of former inmates will be arrested within 3 years, around 50 percent will be reconvicted of a new crime, and roughly 25 percent will be returned to prison for a new sentence (Langan and Levin 2002; Petersilia 2003). Furthermore, Langan and Levin (2002) found that offenders released from prison are responsible for as much as 11 percent of homicides, 10 percent of the robberies, and 12 percent of the burglaries committed in the United States.

Given these figures, public concern over where these inmates will be going and what they will be doing with their time when they get there has resulted in a heightened concern over how well offenders do—or do

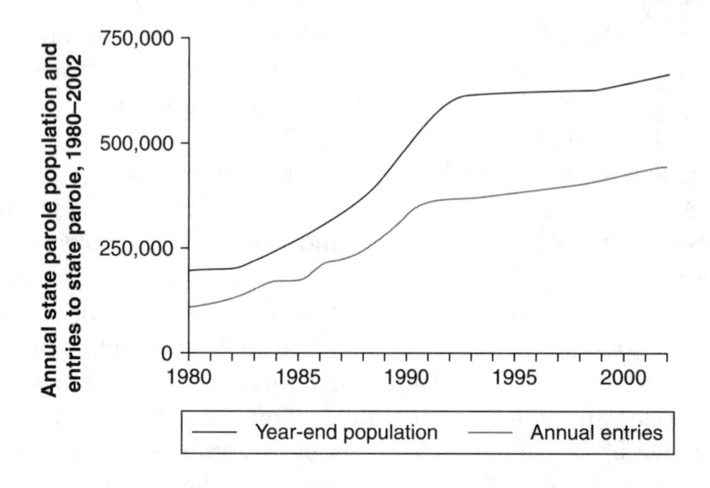

Figure 6.1. Prisoner Reentry Trends, 1980–2002

Source: Bureau of Justice Statistics, 2007b.

not—successfully make the transition into being law-abiding citizens upon release from incarceration. And as "offender reintegration" has become a popular catchphrase in recent years among both correctional scholars and practitioners, even policy makers have started to use the term (Petersilia 2003). Unfortunately, the bulk of policy makers' attention in this area has thus far been devoted to the potential cost savings that may be attributed to releasing inmates, with less concern for how incarceration itself can serve as a barrier to successful offender reintegration.

Ample evidence exists demonstrating the multiple ways in which the experience of incarceration can be criminogenic for offenders. For example, life-course criminological studies have consistently shown how stints of incarceration can interrupt the desistance process for individual offenders by delaying the onset of the age-crime curve (Sampson and Laub 1993). This usually happens because incarceration can disrupt an individual's attachments to the prosocial elements in his or her life (e.g., legitimate employment, marriage; see Laub and Sampson 2003). This trend is particularly pronounced among medium- and low-risk offenders—a fast-growing portion of the inmate population (Spohn 2007)—where evidence from hundreds of studies suggests that the recidivism rates of such incarcerated offenders are actually higher than those who received a less harsh community sanction (Andrews et al. 1990; Lipsey 1992). In short, for a large portion of the inmate population, prison is doing more harm than good.

Our obsession with incarceration has also undermined the potential effectiveness of community alternatives to imprisonment. On the one hand, alternatives to incarceration (e.g., probation/parole supervision, intensive supervision, electronic monitoring/home confinement, short-term boot camps, day reporting centers, drug treatment facilities) are used quite heavily, with nearly 7 million offenders currently under community-based state control (Lab et al. 2008). On the other hand, however, many states have eliminated parole supervision and other aftercare services as policy makers' concern for community corrections has waned in the last couple of decades (Petersilia 1998; Travis and Lawrence 2002).

The dwindling concern for assisting inmates in their attempts to make the transition from the prison to the community cannot be overstated. For example, in many cases an inmate can go from serving out the remainder of his sentence in a supermax prison facility one day—where because of chronic behavioral problems he may have little or no direct contact with another human being for an extended period of time—to the next day being released into the community with no reentry assistance (e.g., housing, transportation, employment) and no conditions of supervision (Kurki and Morris 2001; Pizarro, Stenius, and Pratt 2006). It should come as no surprise that such offenders rarely stay out of trouble for long.

Even inmates who do not pose such a threat to public safety face enormous challenges upon release to the community. At minimum, they are faced with various forms of disenfranchisement that make it more difficult to shed the label of "ex con"—a transition in identity that is, in part, necessary for one to lead a law-abiding life (Maruna 2001). Released inmates also typically face restrictions concerning where they may live (e.g., zoning restrictions for felons generally, specific restrictions for certain types of offenders; public housing eviction for drug convictions), what kinds of job prospects will be available to them (e.g., many positions with state and local agencies will be off-limits), access to student loans for furthering their education (e.g., no federal assistance), and the right to participate in the political process (e.g., voting rights rescinded) (Manza and Uggen 2004; Mosher and Akins 2007).[1]

While some of these restrictions are understandable from a public safety standpoint (e.g., geographic residency restrictions for sex offenders), most of these "collateral consequences" of incarceration were drawn up by policy makers who were stepping over each other to appear tougher on crime than their peers (Manza, Brooks, and Uggen 2004). The problem is that access to and participation in these social institutions are strongly linked to prosocial behavior (Messner and Rosenfeld 2001). The broader concern here therefore relates to how pursuing incarceration strategies to the exclusion of policies aimed at offender reintegration should be viewed as a *threat to public safety,* being that the experience of incarceration does little to reduce offender recidivism rates (MacKenzie 2001).

Consequences of Incarceration for Communities

A fundamental assumption made by advocates of mass incarceration is that imprisonment can, by definition, only serve a positive social function for communities. After all, offenders are bad people; removing bad people from a community leaves only the good people behind—a net social benefit. Simple as that. Yet the relationships surrounding crime, incarceration, and community health are complex. They do not lend themselves to the simple explanation that incarceration can only have a good impact and that no social harm can come from it. Instead, incarceration has a number of negative consequences on particular communities in America.

Incarceration as a Contributor to the Breakdown of Inner-City Communities

It is certainly no secret that communities can be criminogenic, and criminology has a long tradition of cataloguing the community- and neighborhood-level factors that lead to high rates of criminal and deviant behavior (Shaw and McKay 1942; see also Bursik 1988). In particular, hundreds of criminological studies indicate how structural factors such as economic deprivation, family disruption, and residential mobility—particularly when concentrated within communities populated primarily by racial and ethnic minorities—tend to provide the context in which criminal behavior can flourish (Pratt and Cullen 2005). These factors are important because they set the stage for "social disorganization"—that is, the inability of communities to effectively regulate the behavior of residents through informal social control mechanisms (Bursik and Grasmick 1993; Lowenkamp et al. 2003; Sampson and Groves 1989; Sampson et al. 1997).

More specifically, socially disorganized communities experience higher levels of criminal behavior for two general reasons. First, economic deprivation leads to residential mobility as community residents who have the financial means to relocate do so, leaving behind a large underclass who may be biding their time until they too can escape the neighborhood (W. J. Wilson 1987). With such mobility, few residents have a vested interest in the health of the community and therefore withdraw from public and social action (Coleman 1990), including withdrawing from efforts at crime prevention (Putnam 2000). In essence, such communities have very little in the way of "social capital," which refers to a shared set of prosocial values among community residents and a commitment to solve neighborhood problems collectively (see, e.g., Coleman 1988; Hagan 1994).

Second, high levels of family disruption and residential mobility in such communities mean that there are fewer human resources to monitor and supervise the behavior of children. Moreover, effective parenting, including the consistent control and support of child development, is made more difficult under such conditions (Chase-Lansdale et al. 1997; Furstenburg 1993). Such problems have been linked to the development of low self-control in children (Pratt, Turner, and Piquero 2004), which is one of the strongest risk factors for criminal and deviant behavior over the course of one's life (Pratt and Cullen 2000).

It is intuitive, then, that we should draw our inmate population from the same neighborhoods that experience the highest levels of criminal victimization—those that are characterized by social disorganization. After all, the spatial distribution of crime and victimization should, to a large extent, dictate the spatial nature of the response of incarceration. The traditional view of the benefits of incarceration is therefore that criminal offenders are simply bad people. Thus, the net effect of incarceration on any given community should be a positive one, as those who have been exhibiting a negative influence on the community through their criminal behavior are removed and incapacitated (DiIulio 1994; Spelman 1994; J. Q. Wilson 1975). Further, scholars have argued that since crime causes citizens to be fearful of others in their communities, such fear causes citizens to withdraw socially, to disengage from forms of public cooperation, and to disconnect themselves generally from public life, which in turn contributes to the lack of informal control and supervision of neighborhoods—the end result being even higher rates of crime (Skogan 1990). What may be less intuitive, however, is the potential long-term damage that our current incarceration policies may be doing to such communities.

The problem—one that policy makers have been less willing to entertain—is that offenders have complex relationships with the communities in which they live. As Rose and Clear (1998, 442) note, "they may contribute both positively and negatively toward family and neighborhood life." Specifically, many offenders, particularly the drug offenders who represent the bulk of our inmate population, are also parents and neighbors who shift between legal and illegal means of securing income according to the limited opportunity structures that may exist at any given time (Decker and Van Winkle 1996; M. L. Sullivan 1989). If this is true, and offenders are not really "all bad," the net effect of our current method of incarceration that disproportionately affects members of particular American neighborhoods may be, over time, a negative one because of its overall effect on levels of social disorganization in inner-city communities, for three reasons.

First, while it certainly may be true that a "drug offender" has been removed from the community, it may also be true that the primary source of income for a household was removed in the process, therefore plunging a family—and even the community around them—further into economic despair. Research has shown, for example, that patterns of incarceration can alter the socioeconomic composition of neighborhoods by influencing their labor markets (e.g., the pool of potential employees; see Clear, Rose, and Ryder 2001; Rose and Clear 1998). Second, incarceration can exact a serious toll on human relationships when a spouse is imprisoned. In addition to the strain incarceration can place on a marriage (Fishman 1990), which often exacerbates the community-level problem of high rates of family disruption, communities disproportionately affected by incarceration also have fewer males available for the "marriage market" (see Lynch and Sabol 2000). Moreover, families have been shown to partially insulate children living in high-risk neighborhoods from engaging in criminal behavior, and having fewer men who are marriage material inhibits family formation (Sabol and Lynch 2003; Sampson 1987). Finally, incarceration can directly influence a community's level of residential mobility; every person sent to prison came from some neighborhood and every offender released from prison will return to one. This is an inevitability that Todd Clear and colleagues have termed "coercive mobility" (Clear et al. 2003, 33). When these three factors are taken together, inner-city communities may end up experiencing more, not less, social disorganization as a result of the American brand of incarceration.

The purpose of this discussion is not to paint offenders—even nonviolent, drug-only offenders—as model citizens. Many of these individuals may indeed be lousy husbands, absentee fathers, and a general drain on their communities' resources. Such a view does not, however, fully characterize those who comprise our inmate population. They may not be a candidate for your next best friend, but neither are they completely void of virtue, and policies intended to systematically remove them from their communities may, in the long run, do more harm than good. Put simply, when formal social controls (e.g., incarceration) are used aggressively in a community, informal social controls (e.g., families and other social institutions) tend to be less effective at controlling criminal behavior.

Incarceration and Racial Inequality

The United States has a long history of racial discrimination that has extended into virtually every aspect of institutional life, including criminal justice and beyond (C. R. Mann 1993). Even following the abolition of slavery, much of this discrimination was legally sanctioned until just a few decades ago, including the lawful segregation of American citizens in the arenas of education, employment, and housing. One result of this tradition is widespread racial inequality in this country (Blau 1977). Such racial inequality has, in turn, been strongly linked to criminal behavior and criminal victimization (Blau and Blau 1982; McDonald 1976; Pratt and Cullen 2005). The primary theoretical explanation for the inequality–crime relationship is provided by Blau and Blau (p. 126), who argued that the existence of relative deprivation (inequality)—particularly when linked to race—will engender feelings of hostility among disadvantaged groups who may view such inequities as illegitimate and in violation of "the principle that all men are created equal."

Of course, legal changes beginning in the 1950s eliminated certain overt causes of racial inequality (e.g., school desegregation cases such as *Brown v. Board of Education*, 1954; the 1964 Civil Rights Act; the 1965 Voting Rights Act; the 1968 Fair Housing Act). Nevertheless, other forms of *de facto* racial discrimination persist, tied to a larger structural trend that has occurred with regard to the state (A. G. Johnson 2006). In particular, the reinforcement of racial inequality can be seen in how one policy domain has been largely immune from budget cuts in recent decades (incarceration) while another has consistently been on the chopping block (education)—both of which are closely tied to racial dynamics in this nation.

As stated above, state and federal corrections budgets have been growing steadily over time. At the same time, states' contributions to the costs of public education have been shrinking. For example, only Vermont consistently spends around 5% of its total taxable resources on education; the rest of the states spend even less (U.S. Census Bureau 2000). This trend has been most prominent in minority communities, where public schools have become increasingly racially isolated. Kozol's (2005) recent work illustrates this pattern. He found that certain public school districts in New York City were more than 99% racially homogenous. In fact, in one district of 11,000 students, only 26 were white, indicating a segregation rate of 99.8 percent, which led him to conclude that "two tenths of one percentage point now [mark] the difference between legally enforced apartheid in the South of 1954 and socially and economically enforced apartheid in this New York City neighborhood" (p. 9).

This kind of racial isolation is important in this discussion for a number of reasons, not the least of which is that it results in the concentration of economic deprivation within certain communities and, by extension, within schools (W. J. Wilson 1987). As such, research has indicated that racially homogeneous schools dominated by African American students tend to be among the poorest school districts, yet 96 percent of racially homogeneous schools predominated by whites have middle-class majorities (Orfield and Eaton 1996). Racial isolation in schools has, in turn, been linked to lower levels of academic achievement for black students (Grissmer, Flanagan, and Williamson 1998; Guryan 2001; Jencks and Phillips 1998), a finding that is critically important given the strong association between school performance and delinquent behavior in children (McGloin et al. 2004; McGloin and Widom 2001; Ward and Tittle 1994).

Perhaps most important to the present discussion is the recent work by LaFree and Arum (2006) on the effect of racially inclusive education on the risk of incarceration. Their study examined patterns of racial isolation in schools and incarceration rates for all U.S. states dating back to 1930. Controlling for a host of time-stable and time-varying factors that may also influence incarceration rates, their study revealed two key conclusions. First, black students who were educated with a greater proportion of white classmates experienced lower rates of incarceration as adults. This finding was sufficiently robust in that it persisted for those individuals who migrated outside of their state of birth. Second, and consistent with the increases in racial inequality and racial isolation that have occurred over the last three to four decades, the effect of racial inclusiveness in schools on incarceration rates has actually gotten more pronounced over time. In short, as predominantly black schools have worsened in recent years as a result of the increased concentration of economic deprivation in minority communities, so has black citizens' risk of incarceration over their life span.

The increased likelihood of incarceration for citizens of particular racial/ethnic groups itself has negative social consequences. For example, research has indicated that, at the individual level, incarceration is correlated with reduced income earnings (Western, Kling, and Weiman 2001), yet it is possible that this relationship is an artifact of wage stagnation among those with little education or skills in general. Western's (2002) analysis of data from the National Longitudinal Survey of Youth (NLSY), however, confirms this link more clearly. His study examined the effect of incarceration on wage earning in the context of growing inequality in the United States labor market; in essence, his study treated incarceration as a key "life event" that may trigger a process of cumulative disadvantage over the life course. As such, his results reveal that, independent of other factors (e.g., education, work experience, marital status, aggregate labor market characteristics, and local unemployment rates), the experience of incarceration does, in fact, slow wage growth for released prisoners. Thus, mass incarceration over the last few decades has contributed directly to income inequality in this country.

Such inequalities, in turn, once again contribute to the crime problem in America through their effect on the recidivism rates of released inmates. A recent study by Reisig et al. (2007) confirms this notion. Their study of over 34,000 released inmates in the state of Florida began with the premise that most offenders who are released from prison have considerable anxiety about their prospects for successful reintegration; they are provided with little in the way of state assistance upon reentry; and securing legitimate employment is difficult since their stay in prison has severed their ties to the labor market, their work skills have atrophied, and they now face heightened scrutiny and suspicion from potential employers (Visher and Travis 2003). The results of their analysis showed that prisoners released into communities characterized by high levels of racial inequality had higher rates of recidivism (controlling for a host of other individual-level and contextual factors; see also the study by Kubrin and Stewart 2006). In short, their study indicates that certain inmates not only face the normal obstacles to successful reentry into society, but those who are members of economically marginalized groups will also have to contend with being "isolated from employers, health care services, and other institutions that can facilitate law-abiding reentry into society" (Reisig et al., 2007, p. 413).

Taken together, the research studies above reveal a vicious cycle that surrounds economic deprivation, racial inequality, and incarceration. Indeed, economic deprivation and racial inequality are themselves social conditions of communities that are criminogenic (Pratt and Cullen 2005). High crime rates have therefore elicited the criminal justice response of focusing more punitive efforts—from policing all the way through incarceration—in these areas (Cullen and Gilbert 1982; Sherman, Gartin, and Buerger 1989). Nevertheless, such policy responses, however logical or well-intended at the outset, end up perpetuating the cycle of economic deprivation and racial inequality in what are already at-risk communities.

Consequences of Incarceration for Social Institutions

When examined in an international context, it is clear that a society's emphasis on social support is inversely related to its emphasis on social control (Pratt and Godsey 2003). Public funds do not grow on trees, and spending priorities have to be made. Accordingly, as governmental bodies at multiple levels in the United States have emphasized the social control function of the state (e.g., incarceration, along with other areas of criminal justice), they have been at the same time de-emphasizing their public responsibilities in other areas more associated with social support (e.g., education and public health). Put simply, our addiction to incarceration has negative consequences for a number of other social institutions in our society.

Incarceration and Public Health

Prior to the "get tough" movement of the last 30 years, mental illness and substance abuse were treated by policy makers as problems to be dealt with by mental and public health agencies. This practice reflected a long-held belief in this country that "mentally ill" and "criminal" are not the same thing (Staples 1990); as separate problems, then, they required separate solutions. As mental and public health agencies and their services have been either cut back or eliminated in recent decades, the expanded use of incarceration has been called upon to "pick up the slack" in their absence (Blumstein and Beck 1999). The result is that a substantial portion of the inmate population is composed of nonserious, drug-only offenders (Austin and Irwin 2001), many of whom have serious mental and physical health problems.

For example, although estimates vary, evidence suggests that up to 80 percent of incarcerated inmates in the United States have a substance abuse problem (see Table 6.1; see also Clear et al. 2006; Mosher and Akins 2007). While it may be a commonly held belief that such offenders typically commit a range of other, more serious offenses to fuel their drug habits (e.g., robbery, residential burglary), the research presented in Table 6.2 indicates otherwise (see, e.g., B. Johnson et al. 2000). Instead, most of these drug-only offenders are just that: addicts who have been popped multiple times for possession or have failed to stay clean under community supervision (Austin and Irwin 2001). It is therefore the disease of their addiction—one that is closely tied to their mental and physical health—that has landed them in prison.[2] Yet rather than bring a health-related solution to what is obviously a health-related problem, our current drug policy has morphed into one that instead treats chemical addiction as a criminal justice problem. In essence, by applying the wrong solution, we virtually ensure the failure of our correctional system to "solve" the drug problem.

And it's not just drugs. Other work notes that a sizeable percentage of inmates suffer from an array of psychological disorders, including schizophrenia, depression, bipolar disorder, and antisocial personality disorder (Hamilton et al. 2006; C. J. Sullivan, Veysey, and Dorangrichia 2003), many of which co-occur with inmates' drug problems (Huntington, Moses, and Veysey 2005). For example, New York's Riker's Island jail now houses over 3,000 mentally ill inmates, making it the country's largest psychiatric facility (Winerip 1999). Furthermore, evidence suggests that 25 percent of the nation's inmate population has been diagnosed with

Table 6.1 Drug Use by State Prisoners, 1997 and 2004

	Percentage of Inmates Who Had Ever Used Drugs	
Type of Drug	*2004*	*1997*
Any drug	83	83
Marijuana	78	77
Cocaine/crack	47	49
Heroin/opiates	23	24
Depressants	21	24
Stimulants	29	28
Hallucinogens	33	29

Source: Bureau of Justice Statistics 2006b.

Table 6.2 Percentage of Prison and Jail Inmates Who Committed Their Present Offense to Get Money for Drugs

	Local Jail Inmates	*State Prisoners*	*Federal Prisoners*
Offense	*2002*	*2004*	*2004*
Total	16.4	16.6	18.4
Violent	8.0	9.8	14.8
Property	26.9	30.3	10.6
Drugs	24.8	26.4	25.3
Public-order	5.2	6.9	6.8

Source: Bureau of Justice Statistics 2005, 2006b.

attention-deficit hyperactivity disorder (ADHD) (Foley, Carlton, and Howell 1996), a factor that has been linked to criminal behavior (Pratt et al. 2002), and that 50 to 80 percent exhibit a significant number of ADHD-related symptoms (Richardson 2000). It is clear, then, that the state's shift in emphasis from social service to social control has resulted in new responsibilities for our correctional system that extend well beyond the task of administering punishment. It is also clear that, aside from administering pharmacological cocktails to inmates to keep them docile—a practice particularly popular for dealing with female inmates (Morash et al. 1994)—prisons are simply ill-equipped to effectively treat the spectrum of mental health problems facing the inmate population.

Moreover, as sentences have stiffened in recent decades, resulting in more inmates being incarcerated for longer periods of time, we are now facing an increasingly aging population of prison inmates. To be sure, the proportion of the inmate population over 50 years of age has risen steadily with the get-tough movement's constellation of policies designed to incarcerate more offenders (Auerhahn 2002). The "graying" of the inmate population is problematic for two reasons. First, maintaining an increasingly older inmate population does little to enhance public safety. Empirical studies in the life-course tradition in criminology have consistently shown the presence of an age-crime curve, indicating that individuals exhibit less and less criminal behavior as they get older (Gottfredson and Hirschi 1990). Since this process known as "desistance" tends to begin in the mid-20s, by the time individuals are in their 50s they generally pose little risk to the public (Farrington 1986). Second, older inmates require much more in the way of health care costs relative to their younger counterparts, largely because of the degenerative consequences of high rates of infectious diseases, such as HIV and multidrug-resistant tuberculosis, among the inmate population in general (Auerhahn 2002). Taken together, this evidence suggests that it may no longer be appropriate to view prisons merely as prisons, but also as drug treatment centers, mental health facilities, hospitals, and nursing homes.

Incarceration and the Privatization of Punishment

A final consequence of our addiction to incarceration has emerged out of the intersection of two interrelated developments: the rapid growth in the inmate population and the rapid decline in the degree to which policy makers seem to care about what happens to inmates once they are incarcerated (see Feeley and Simon 1992). Although lawmakers tend to view this large group of citizens as generally "undeserving" (Hallinan 2001), they are certainly an expensive bunch. How, then, can those in charge of punishment policy continue to get tougher and tougher—and incarcerate more and more Americans—when state budgets are strapped? One answer has been to privatize the practice of punishment.

Private involvement in criminal justice in America is certainly not a new phenomenon. Our entrepreneurial legacy stretches back to colonial Western Europe—and to England in particular—where merchant shippers profited significantly in the business of punishment through the use of transportation of inmates to North America and other mid-Atlantic colonies (not to mention Australia; see Ekirch 1987). The money to be made in punishment did not stop there, however: even Jeremy Bentham, the noted Enlightenment thinker and brains behind the Panopticon prison design, lobbied assiduously (yet ultimately unsuccessfully) to obtain an exclusive contract to build and operate a private, self-financing prison, from which he fully expected to become rich as a result (Semple 1993). Moreover, in the United States, virtually all facets of the punishment apparatus relied heavily on private innovation throughout the 18th and 19th centuries, including policing, bail, community supervision, and prison (Feeley 2002). The public monopoly on punishment, by comparison, is a rather recent social phenomenon.

In its more current form, correctional privatization in the United States grew out of the Reagan-era mantra of the managerial brilliance of the private sphere—better (or at least comparable) correctional services at a lower cost to the state (W. A. Donohue 1985; Hutto 1988; Logan 1990; Mullen 1985; Steelman and Harms 1986). As a result of these promises, nearly every state in the United States relies on the private sector, in some capacity, for correctional services (Perrone and Pratt 2003). To that end, much of the research and public debate surrounding prison privatization has focused on issues such as cost-effectiveness and quality of correctional service provision, where the best available evidence indicates that the private sphere does not have all that much to brag about (Perrone and Pratt 2003; Pratt and Maahs 1999). Cost-effectiveness and quality correctional services do not appear, therefore, to be the exclusive domain of American private enterprise (DiIulio 1991). Scholars such as John DiIulio (1988) early on argued that prison privatization merely amounted to an attempt by the state to evade one of its core responsibilities (the punishment of citizens) by limiting its liabilities.

Recent discussions have focused more closely on the normative problems associated with injecting the profit motive into punishment practice (Ogle 1999; Reisig and Pratt 2000). In particular, the political realities inherent in a punishment-for-profit framework (e.g., the need to generate profits that can be demonstrated to corporate shareholders)—and the ethical concerns they raise—have themselves contributed to our incarceration boom in a number of important ways. Examined in this light, inmates are no longer viewed as citizens who will eventually be released into our communities, but are instead viewed as commodities or, as Schwartz and Nurge (2004, 133) point out, "producers of income to be fought over." The fact that inmates can now be bought, sold, traded, and transferred like any other product has created and sustained the "corrections-commercial complex" for a number of years now (Lilly and Knepper 1993, 156; see also Lilly and Deflem 1996; Shichor 1995).

One of the most salient consequences of this trend (at least with regard to prison growth) is that private corporations now spend considerable time and money lobbying policy makers to increase the punitiveness of sanctions in an effort to generate more inmates who will stay in prison for longer periods of time (Hallett 2002). There is nothing conspiratorial about this practice, and lobbying efforts by corporations seem to be a fact of American political life when it comes to pharmaceutical products, corporate tax breaks, and greenhouse gas emissions. When dealing with citizens' freedom, however, many scholars have expressed concern over ethical legitimacy of allowing powerful private firms to lobby state legislatures to extend prison sentences or limit parole releases so that the prisons they own could maintain a stable (or, better yet, growing) population of inmates (see Schwartz and Nurge 2004).

Examples certainly abound. For instance, Biewen (2002) found that both the Corrections Corporation of America (CCA) and Wackenhut—two of the largest private prison firms in the United States—have actively financed legislators in key committee positions to create and push legislation that would stiffen prison sentences (see also Cheung 2002). Furthermore, a report released by the National Institute on Money in State Politics (2002) showed that in southern states alone, private prison companies donated over $1.1 million to political candidates—mostly to well-placed, powerful incumbents—and were rewarded with financially lucrative contracts in return. Even academics have been pulled into the mess, such as when University of Florida professor Charles W. Thomas, a long-time advocate for CCA's private prisons, was fined $20,000 by the Florida State Ethics Board. It turned out that he had made millions of (undisclosed) dollars in his capacity as an "advisor" to CCA while publishing a number of articles extolling the bountiful benefits of private prisons (see the discussion in Geis et al. 1999).

But the problem of private involvement in punishment might run even deeper. As Feeley (2002) has recently argued, the philosophy of the minimal state that tends to underlie the private contracting of public services (i.e., one that places faith in the efficiency of the market) turns the scope of social control on its head. Instead of reducing the size of the state, Feeley argues that efforts to privatize criminal justice in general—and corrections in particular—have in fact expanded the reach of criminal sanctions. For example, driven by the "get tough" political ethic, the United States now houses nearly half of its secure, custodial juvenile offenders in private institutions (Winston and Pratt 1999); for-profit treatment facilities for juveniles and adults have mushroomed—most of which were created for voluntary admissions but now receive offenders sentenced from the courts (some of which explicitly market their services to those who have yet to be convicted so that participation in treatment will be viewed favorably at adjudication); and new forms of electronic surveillance have all extended the hold of social control.

It is clear, therefore, that getting tough has been politically profitable for corrections policy stakeholders in a number of different ways. Our overflowing inmate population "works" for a number of key players in the corrections policy arena, many of whom have a vested interest in maintaining the status quo of an unreasonably harsh correctional system. And it is not just policy makers—corporate America has recognized the money to be made in the prison business. A short list of prison-based financial ventures includes the pay phones that both AT&T and MCI place inside of facilities to soak up revenue from inmates' collect calls, while others such as Proctor & Gamble and Pillsbury reap enormous profits each year through contracts with state departments of correction. Even Helen Curtis Industries went so far as to set up a booth for themselves at the annual meeting of the American Correctional Association in an effort to market their shampoo to prisons (Hallinan 2001).

Given the money to be made, at best, current conventional wisdom among policy makers is that well-conceived correctional practices aimed at the reintegration of offenders, while certainly good for communities, are bad for business. At worst, they are a threat to the personal and political livelihood of policy makers and their benefactors. Either way, the money to be made in the prison industry serves as a significant—although not insurmountable—barrier to substantive change in corrections policy.

Summary

Taken together, the work presented in this chapter indicates that the social and political disenfranchisement of an entire class of citizenry, the systematic removal of a large portion of a neighborhood's residents, and the increasing racial isolation of members of minority communities are each tied, in some way, to the practice of incarceration in this country, particularly when viewed in the context of the profits to be made in punishment. It is certainly questionable whether these were the intended or unintended outcomes of those in charge of the business of incarceration (e.g., see Reiman 2004). Regardless of intentions, however, what first needs to be recognized is that policies have consequences; political developments that occur in the areas of incarceration, health care, and education all have implications for other policy domains, including criminal justice.

The purpose of this chapter was to highlight the consequences of our current practice of incarceration. At minimum, the primary goal here was to show how the simple view that imprisoning bad people can only have a good outcome is fallacious. Instead, policies that get developed in an effort to purportedly fight crime (e.g., mandatory minimum sentences, elimination of parole release and other reentry services, and so on) can end up, in the long run, worsening the social conditions that breed crime in the first place. What we need to do, then, is reconsider the way we think about crime control policy in general and corrections policy in particular—a task for the final chapter, which follows.

Notes

1. This roster of collateral consequences can be viewed primarily as resulting from a felony conviction, not incarceration per se. Nevertheless, each of these policy-based limitations certainly applies to offenders released from prison.

2. It should be noted that the notion of a chemical addiction being a disease, not simply the result of a simple and purposive choice on the part of an offender, is not universally accepted among policy makers. It is, however, the designation most consistent with mental health disorders among substance abuse treatment scholars (Ketcham and Asbury 2000).

Seven

Conclusions and Recommendations

The purpose of this book was not to advocate a massive decarceration movement. To be sure, James Q. Wilson's (1975, 235) famous edict that "wicked people exist. Nothing avails except to set them apart from innocent people" rings much more true than many left-leaning criminologists would be willing to admit in public. Prisons exist for a reason: some people simply cannot function according to our society's rules, and the harm offenders inflict on society is incredibly damaging and is in no way the figment of conservative policy makers' collective imagination. Expecting the state to use prisons for the protection of society is understandable on the part of American citizens (Cullen et al. 2000).

Prisons also represent a fundamental tool for providing retribution for criminal offenses. Much of this book has focused on the perceived utility of punishment, that is, the extent to which the existence and use of prisons reduces crime—a shaky proposition at best. Nevertheless, to the extent that punishment is based on "desert" rather than utility, prisons are certainly necessary social institutions. For example, even if we could make a serial child molester a functioning member of society through rehabilitation programs, there still remains the normative question of whether or not we should be in the business of doing so in the first place. This is questionable, and such ethical concerns about why we *should* punish lawbreakers are important ones that have unfortunately been lost in a public debate that has increasingly focused on the cold economics of crime control.

The bottom line, however, is that the potential retributive properties of prisons have taken a back seat to a failed promise that we can build our way out of the crime problem. Yet, the assumption of crime control through incarceration does not seem to be going anywhere. A recent statement by a crime control "expert" has emphatically claimed that "punishment works—and the United States has barely tried it" (Methvin 2006, 345). Others agree and go even further to contend that not only does punishment (in particular, prison) "work," it is even cost-effective (DiIulio and Piehl 1991). Thus, there are still a few corrections "scholars" out there who continue to tout the message that prisons are an effective crime control bargain.

The purpose of this book has been to point out the sources of misinformation that have been used in support of those arguments. Thus, anyone still wanting to cling to these falsehoods would need to either ignore the mountain of empirical evidence that indicates otherwise or accept the evidence as valid and decide to spout disingenuous rhetoric about it anyway. My hope is that correctional policy makers, when faced with valid information on the subject, will choose the reasonable path. What is necessary, then, is a more evidence-based approach to crime control policy in general, and to responsible corrections policy in particular.

Rethinking Crime Control Policy

Effective crime control policy—that which may provide the substantive benefit of actually reducing crime as opposed to the symbolic benefit of merely making it look like we are trying—will first require a general shift in philosophy. In particular, we need to begin the process of moving away from the get-tough movement we have been mired in for the last few decades. This shift will not be easy; the get-tough punitive womb has begat such fine crime control offspring as Maricopa County, Arizona's "tent city" (where the county sheriff boasts that the dogs held at the facility are treated better than the human charges under his control), MTV's redux of the previously ineffective "scared straight" program (where juvenile offenders are invited to a day in prison spent with inmates with a life sentence, who threaten them, yell at them, and attempt to scare them with tales of gang rape and mayhem), and the revival of the chain gang in the South. It is obvious that these policy approaches have both political and media appeal. For policy makers, such programs have the veneer of getting tough and they're cheap; the media like them because they simply make good TV. Nevertheless, collectively they have achieved little to nothing in the way of crime reduction.

Instead, effective crime control policy first requires targeting the factors that are actually related to crime. Given the discussion in Chapter 6, what this means is that policies aimed at ameliorating the effects of economic deprivation and family disruption—especially in community contexts with large proportions of racial minorities—are likely to have a significant impact on crime reduction. These policies could come in the form of social support efforts on the part of public or private entities to help families stay stable in the face of economic hardship, such as early intervention programs for at-risk families and youth; financial, housing, and transportation assistance; and quality health care and education programs (Currie 1998). Some scholars have also suggested that directed efforts at job creation, systematic efforts to upgrade working wages, and greater support for labor organization in communities characterized by economic deprivation may help to reduce crime (W. J. Wilson 1996).

It is important to note that these approaches to crime control do not require a radical transformation of the existing social structure. For example, Pratt and Godsey's (2003) cross-national analysis of 46 countries found that those that devoted a greater portion of their GDP to health care and education experienced significantly lower rates of violent crime (in particular, homicides). Furthermore, a greater emphasis on supporting such social institutions lessened the influence of economic inequality on crime rates, in that nations with high levels of social support could still experience relatively low homicide rates even in the face of high levels of inequality (like the levels we see in the United States). Thus, increases in levels of social support in these areas are capable of producing concomitant reductions in crime, even in the absence of a social and economic revolution—the impossible task that policy makers have often invoked for ignoring the recommendations of academics. Still, this approach does require a shift in a fundamental assumption of human behavior, to one that says crime may be more effectively reduced by doing something *for* a person rather than doing something *to* a person (see, e.g., the discussion in Cullen, Wright, and Chamlin 1999).

On that note, perhaps the most fundamental implication of the work discussed here is that effective crime control policies must extend beyond the walls (both literally and figuratively) of the criminal justice system. It is easy for both the public and policy makers to assume that each policy domain, from welfare to education and from health care to economics, is an island unto itself that does not affect, and is not affected by, the others (Galbraith 1996). The reality is that effective crime control policies are more likely to be articulated once policy makers embrace the notion that the decisions they make in one policy arena have repercussions for the others. Accordingly, adopting a more progressive crime control policy agenda that specifically targets the multiplicity of negative effects associated with concentrated disadvantage is much more likely to result in a substantial reduction in crime. In short, embracing this approach will require a conversion in our crime control faith—one where thinking about a complex problem (crime) in a complex way is no longer a sin.

Rethinking Corrections Policy

It would be ridiculous to even discuss potential changes to corrections policy without an explicit focus on how we should deal with drug offending and drug offenders. Accordingly, the development of rational, evidence-based corrections policy should begin with a shift in our view of drug use to seeing it as a public health—as opposed to a criminal justice—problem. This will be no easy task: the "war on drugs" is well entrenched in this country and is reinforced by both criminal justice policy and practice. A prime example of our dependence on viewing the drug problem exclusively as a crime problem can be seen in Worrall's (2001) recent study of the budgetary practices of over 1,400 local law enforcement agencies around the country. He found that many agencies depended significantly on revenue generated from civil asset forfeiture, which is the seizure and forfeiture of property connected with drug crimes, as a major source of their organization's annual budgets. Thus, adhering to the war on drugs philosophy has become profitable for law enforcement, providing a strong disincentive to take a more progressive look at drug policy (i.e., one that reacts to drug use with something other than arrest and incarceration).

Nevertheless, we already have a good start with the advent and proliferation of drug courts, which recognize the need for an approach to the drug problem that is not purely punitive. As of the turn of this century, over 700 drug courts were in operation around the country, most of which were created under the assumption that treatment, as opposed to mere punishment, is a more appropriate sanction for drug offenders (Taxman and Bouffard 2005). And although the results of the empirical evaluations of drug courts remain somewhat mixed, the general trend in the literature is that drug court graduates have lower recidivism rates compared to nongraduates and those under standard probation supervision (see Goldkamp, White, and Robinson 2001; Shaffer 2006).

The expanded use of drug courts has occurred on the heels of a larger call among corrections policy advocates to reinvest in community corrections. After all, most of the offenders subject to state control are under some form of community sanction, hence the importance of taking community corrections seriously for the sake of reducing levels of criminal victimization (see the discussion in Petersilia 1998; see also DiIulio 1999). Furthermore, there is ample evidence that a variety of community sanctions provide a better context for correctional treatment and are less likely to disrupt offenders' networks of social capital, which in turn may increase the likelihood that an offender will refrain from recidivism (Holtfreter, Reisig, and Morash 2004; Lutze 1998).

Nevertheless, it is important to note that not all treatment programs are created equal (Gendreau and Ross 1987). More specifically, Izzo and Ross (1990, 141) concluded that "[w]hether a program works depends on who does what to whom, why, and where." What makes an effective correctional treatment program, however, is not a mystery; a set of three "principles of effective correctional treatment" have been identified and empirically validated (see Gendreau 1996). First, the risk level of the offender should be matched to the intensity of the program. That is, higher-risk offenders should be placed in more intensive programs while lower-risk offenders should receive less intensive services. Second, correctional treatment programs should target factors that are actually related to recidivism such as antisocial attitudes, family, peer associations, and substance abuse. Alternatively, programs that merely target "commonsense" risk factors that are nevertheless weakly related to recidivism (e.g., self-esteem or fear of push-ups in correctional "boot camps") are unlikely to significantly reduce lawbreakers' propensities to reoffend. Finally, treatment programs should match the offender characteristics to therapist characteristics and type of treatment. For example, factors such as offenders' IQ and level of anxiety may render them more or less responsive to particular types of treatment interventions. Correctional programs that follow these principles achieve the greatest reduction in recidivism (on average, 30 to 50 percent) relative to all other types of interventions, including the politically popular, yet ineffective, get-tough approaches (Palmer 1992; Pratt 2002).

The key, then, is to reframe the correctional policy debate—at least with regard to correctional rehabilitation and treatment—in a way that highlights the role such an approach can play in controlling crime. Put differently, if such an approach can be demonstrated to enhance public safety, and the empirical record of well-crafted correctional treatment programs has demonstrated just that, policy makers who choose to reject such an approach would be forced to adopt a pro-victimization platform. In short, even policy makers (and citizens) seem to have no trouble believing that good people can be "turned bad" (e.g., by drugs, hanging out with deviant peers, and the like). It's time we embraced the notion—and the reality—that the opposite is also true. But how do we get started on the path of changing minds about crime and punishment? That is the subject of the remainder of this chapter.

Reconnecting Research and Policy

A number of criminologists have commented on the apparent gulf that exists between academic researchers and public policy makers (Currie 1998; Gottfredson 1982). This may not be surprising since funding available for large-scale policy evaluations is limited, and even universities tend to downplay the prestige of applied policy research (see, e.g., the discussion in Mears 2007). While these explanations are certainly true, policy analysts have instead explained this communication problem in terms of the indifference of academic researchers to the political constituencies to which policy makers are devoted (Weimer and Vining 1992). Although perhaps this explanation is somewhat oversimplified (Beckett 1997), it seems to contain a nugget of truth. Criminologists have criticized the utility of the get-tough movement in criminal justice since as far back as the late 1960s (Clear 1994), only to have their warnings dismissed by policy makers as being politically unrealistic given the pervasive conservative culture in American society (Gordon 1990). The constant threat of having one's policy proposals ridiculed, thwarted, or otherwise ignored by policy makers has even caused some of the more influential criminologists in the field to withdraw from the policy debate altogether and to advocate a retreat into the relative safety of the ivory tower (Cressey 1978).

It is important to note, however, that academic research is not incapable of influencing criminal justice policy. Since the 1970s, political pundits have often heeded the advice of certain criminologists who have advocated the adoption of get-tough policies while at the same time condemning the more progressive crime control agenda traditionally championed by social scientists (for examples of such questionable, yet influential, criminology, see DiIulio 1994; Murray 1984). Given the level of influence afforded to these policy advocates in recent years, it appears that the inability of many criminologists to reroute the punitive direction that criminal justice policy has taken over the last few decades may not simply be attributable to policy makers' unwillingness to listen to the message being sent by academics. Perhaps a more troubling contribution to the "knowledge gap" in this context has to do with an inability on the part of criminologists to "speak truth to power" (Wildavsky 1979, 15) in an understandable, politically savvy way (see also Bobrow and Dryzek 1987).

To that end, hundreds of peer-reviewed journal articles appear each year in criminal justice and criminology journals, many of which have direct implications for corrections policy, yet it still seems as though such works—and the scholars that produce them—continue to be snubbed by policy makers. Some, including noted criminologist and long-time member of the National Council on Crime and Delinquency, James Austin (2003, 557), have even gone so far as to label criminology "irrelevant." The central problem—at least according to Austin (p. 558)—is that criminologists produce little in the way of quality research. Put more forcefully, he describes the evidence we produce as "scant," our methods "dismal," our body of published work "shoddy and superficial," and our conclusions generally equivocal.

If Austin is right, this is particularly damaging since, in recent years, criminal justice policy makers in general—and corrections policy makers in particular—have begun to embrace the notion of "evidence-based" policy making (MacKenzie 2000; see also Eskridge 2005; Jones and Pratt, 2008; Mears 2007; Perrone and Pratt 2003; Sherman et al. 1997; Stolz 2002). The premise of this approach is that policies should be developed according to the best available empirical evidence on the subject. If we have no firm empirical evidence to offer policy makers, as Austin contends, how then can academics engage themselves in this opportunity? The problem, however, is that Austin is incorrect; the research presented in this book alone is a testament to the inaccuracy of Austin's pessimism. Instead, the irrelevance of which he speaks—whether real or imagined—has less to do with the quality of the work produced by criminologists and more to do with the way that knowledge gets *communicated* to policy makers by criminologists.

In short, the scholars charged with the task of producing the most methodologically rigorous empirical research relevant to our understanding of "what works" in crime control have themselves contributed to the chasm between research and public policy. Indeed, policy makers' tendency toward simple (and often inaccurate) explanations of crime, which, in turn, tend to lead to equally simple (and equally inaccurate) crime control solutions, can no longer be considered a mere reflection of their unwillingness to consider the best available evidence. The academic community must make a number of changes concerning how we present and disseminate the knowledge we produce through our research. Only then may we fully expect policy makers to take our advice seriously. To that end, I conclude this book with four suggestions for narrowing the gap between scholarly research and corrections policy (for an elaboration of these points, see Pratt 2008).

1. Disseminate the Knowledge

First, when it comes to "getting the word out" concerning the results of our research, criminologists need to do a better job of self-promotion. Unlike, say, the American Medical Association, where socially important research published in their flagship journal (the *Journal of the American Medical Association*) is marketed heavily to the major news organizations, criminologists tend to take a much more reserved approach and almost consciously eschew publicity for our work. Instead, we generally prefer to talk to each other about the research we publish in our rather obscure, peer-reviewed outlets and to hobnob in national conferences discussing our latest findings, but rarely do we actively seek out those not privy to the scholarly secret handshake to make our results known more widely. Academics themselves are rarely able to keep up with the production of new research in the various journals of the discipline, so why would we expect policy makers to be eagerly waiting by the mailbox for the new issue of *Justice Quarterly* or *Criminology* to come? Thus, if policy makers aren't familiar with our work, it isn't necessarily their fault—it's ours. This is not to say that we need to push our research with a media blitz worthy of the latest Hollywood darling, but we can—and should—take advantage of the media services available at our universities and pressure our professional organizations to be more aggressive with the public dissemination of the results of the studies published in our own flagship journals.

This process has, to a certain extent, already begun in criminal justice and criminology. For example, in 2001 the American Society of Criminology began publishing a new peer-reviewed journal called *Criminology and Public Policy*. The mission of this journal is to "strengthen the role of research findings in the formulation of crime and justice policy by publishing empirically based, policy focused articles." This journal forces authors to explicitly address the policy implications of their work, a public relations firm has been retained to help disseminate the findings contained in the journal, and its readership has been growing ever since its inception. Another development is the Crime and Justice Group of the Campbell Collaboration (see www.campbellcollaboration.org), which is involved in the ongoing process of continually reviewing and interpreting the social scientific research on the effectiveness of criminal justice policies.

These efforts represent a great start, but it still remains to be seen how much of this work makes its way into the hands of policy makers. In that vein, some scholars have called for the creation of criminal justice policy councils—which would bring together criminal justice practitioners, scholars, and policy makers—that would serve both research and policy-deliberation functions at the state level (e.g., see the discussion in Mears 2007). Others have called for the development of university-based institutes or centers that would serve a similar function (Cullen 2005). Either way, much of the onus will still be on the shoulders of the scholars who produce the work as opposed to exclusively relying upon policy councils, university institutes, or the professional organizations to which they may belong.

2. Avoid Academic Jargon

Second, as scholars we need to discuss our work in a language that can be interpreted by the policy-making audience. Academic training has its own set of odd incentives, one of which involves the cultural pressure to develop a new language. Early on in graduate school, we leave behind our primary language (the one that noncriminologists and policy makers use all the time) in an effort to gain command over a new, and necessary, secondary language—one where words like *heteroscedasticity, semiparametric modeling,* and *spatial autocorrelation* all make sense. In the process, the secondary language becomes the primary language, at which time the speech patterns employed by academics hit the ears of policy makers as self-indulgent, career-nerd gibberish. The challenge for criminologists, then, is to discuss the results of our work—even if they are complex—in a way that appreciates that complexity but does not rely on the crutch of academic jargon. This isn't "dumbing it down," but quite the opposite: explaining our results to intelligent people who are not themselves criminologists. Policy makers can handle it, but the responsibility is on us to move beyond the safety of the academic nest to give our work a chance to succeed or fail in the "real world."

An example can be found in Weisburd, Einat, and Kowalski's (2008) evaluation of New Jersey's MUSTER program, which was published in *Criminology and Public Policy.* The results from their randomized experimental research design reaffirm the notion that the threat of sanctions—the staple of the get-tough movement—tends to work best when the goals of the sanction are more modest. As opposed to placing faith in the "general" effectiveness of writing laws to control offenders' behavior, their study demonstrates how *particular* types of sanction threats (the threat of incarceration) can bring about a *particular* type of prosocial behavior (paying fines) for a *particular* segment of the offender population (low-risk probationers).[1]

What is important here is that there is nothing simple about randomized experimental research designs; they inevitably involve managing a number of complex methodological issues (sampling and assignment protocols) and successfully navigating the political waters (e.g., securing judicial compliance with researchers' methodological requests). Nevertheless, Weisburd et al.'s (2008) discussion of the results of their work didn't get bogged down in the language of statistics, but rather the study concluded clearly that, for low-risk probationers sentenced with a fine, the looming threat of jail time for noncompliance "works" (see also the discussion in Pratt 2008). This is precisely the kind of straightforward translation of social science for policy that criminologists would do well to emulate.

3. Enough With the Wishy-Washy!

Third, criminologists need to stop being equivocal about what the research indicates. Few things render criminologists more intellectually impotent than being wishy-washy about what the research says about a given subject. Of course, in certain areas where the research is new or underdeveloped, caution concerning which policies should or should not be considered is understandable. In corrections research, however, we have hundreds of studies in particular areas that clearly point to what does and does not "work" for reducing crime (see, e.g., Andrews et al. 1990; Cullen and Gendreau 2000; Dowden and Andrews 1999, 2000, 2004; Gendreau and Ross 1987; Lipsey 1992, 1995; Pratt 2002; Pratt and Cullen 2005; Sherman et al. 1997). Furthermore, as scholars, when we publish our work it means that we've convinced at least three anonymous reviewers and the editor, during what can be a vicious and humbling process, that what we've found is not some methodological artifact but is rather a reflection of some enduring social reality. Accordingly, we should not balk at the validity of our own work when relating it to policy makers. We need to have some faith that this body of research wasn't an accident so that we can speak with unambiguous confidence when asked about the likelihood of success for a particular corrections policy proposal.

Such a sentiment may, however, be interpreted by some as being inconsistent with criminologists' professional norm of cautious deliberation. My suggestion here is not that we as scholars should abandon the complexity we know exists in our subject area, but rather to reverse the order in which that complexity is presented to whomever we are speaking. To illustrate this point, outside of the classroom, academics will often treat policy-related questions as an opportunity to educate citizens, the media, or policy makers about various nuances of criminological research. In the form of a lecture, scholars will typically lead off by noting the complex gray areas in the research and then end with a more definitive summary statement (perhaps it is the flair for the dramatic that leads professors to keep the audience in suspense until delivering the broad "lesson" at the end). This approach would be easily translated into a message that both the media and policy makers could use if the order of the message were flipped. If scholars would lead with the more certain (and brief) response to a question, and then offer their qualifying remarks, our words would have more impact.

So, say that one were asked the following question by, for example, a reporter: "The state wants to expand the use of boot camp prisons; will this 'work' for reducing crime?" My advice here is to avoid the temptation to answer it by going directly to nuance (e.g., "Its success may vary according to what kinds of offenders would be sentenced to such a facility, what other alternatives are being considered by the state, and how one might define whether something "works."); at the same time, resist the urge to redefine the question (e.g., "It isn't so much whether it 'works,' but rather how well it may do relative to some other sentencing option."). Instead, approach it with something like this: "No, we have no firm empirical research that would indicate a general reduction in crime as a result of boot camps." After that (more definitive) statement is delivered, one can feel as free as one wants to follow up with qualifications and appeals to complexity—the reporter will still be listening. Don't be afraid that your single-word response of "no" will be the only thing printed (they're after more than that); the nuance we know and love will make it in there.

4. Understand Policy Makers' Incentives

Finally, we need to present our work in a way that policy makers would not find politically threatening should they choose to follow our advice. Take, for example, the case for advocating the practice and philosophy of correctional rehabilitation. Policy makers have historically been hesitant to embrace such an approach over concerns, at least in part, about coming off as soft on crime (i.e., that rehabilitation isn't really "punishment"; see Cullen and Gilbert 1982; Garland 1990). If, however, the body of work demonstrating the effectiveness of correctional rehabilitation strategies relative to other approaches (e.g., mindlessly "getting tough") is presented in a way that emphasizes the role of rehabilitation in enhancing public safety, policy makers are more likely to get on board. After all, what sane policy maker would be willing to stump on a pro-victimization platform? In short, getting tough is itself an implicit appeal to public safety; scholars would do well, then, to recognize this reality and work within it as opposed to rejecting it outright and becoming marginalized in the policy-making process as a result of doing so.

The first step toward accomplishing this is to recognize that both American citizens and policy makers are extremely utilitarian. We are all quick to ask the "what's in it for me" question. At the risk of oversimplifying things, policy makers are concerned with reelection, criminal justice practitioners are concerned with their jobs, and citizens are concerned for their safety and the safety of their children. The sooner that scholars recognize these incentives—and how they are all intertwined with each other—the more likely they will be in a position to speak to such groups in a way that is consistent with the incentives that motivate them.

Some Final Advice for Students and Responsible Citizens

Most people will not become criminologists themselves. The Academy of Criminal Justice Sciences and the American Society of Criminology—the two primary professional organizations for criminologists in this country—boast a combined membership of roughly 5,000 scholars. Accordingly, the ability to separate reliable from unreliable information will be critical if criminal justice/criminology students (from the hundreds of college- and university-based criminal justice and criminology programs nationwide) and responsible United States citizens are to have a positive effect on punishment policy. To that end, I offer two pieces of advice.

First, adopt for yourself the identity of being a critical consumer of information. Don't be merely dismissive (not all information is bad), which is an easy trap to fall into when distrust of policy makers and government organizations is high. It gets even easier in the face of evidence that the federal government has recently done everything from withholding research funding to censoring (or even blocking the release of) the research produced by scholars whose conclusions are at odds with the current administration's political preferences (Mooney 2006). Instead, simply assume that not all information is created equal. For example, the peer-reviewed published work produced in universities—where scholars have no direct investment in a particular outcome (or are at least less motivated by financial benefits to be inclined toward one)—will typically be of higher quality than the work that emerges from political agencies.

Second, I strongly urge all readers to follow the advice of Francis T. Cullen, the former president of the American Society of Criminology. For nearly three decades, he has encouraged his students at the University of Cincinnati to recognize that "the world is multivariate." To be sure, we need to get comfortable with thinking about crime, punishment, and corrections in complex ways. Regardless of how emotionally or politically attractive simple explanations of these problems may be, and how dependent upon them we may have become, they're a major reason behind why we're in this pickle in the first place. Breaking an addiction is hard work; admitting that we have a problem may the first step toward recovery.

Parting Shots

These sets of suggestions aren't necessarily fool-proof blueprints for how scholars, students, practitioners, and citizens can get their voices heard where previously they had not. At minimum, however, they should provide criminologists with a different way of looking at how to disseminate their work in a way that increases their chances of making a difference in the policy arena. In the end, the studies we publish should amount to more than, at best, tenure and promotion fodder for scholars and, at worst, refrigerator art for our own amusement. Changing the direction of corrections policy will not be easy, and results from efforts to do so may not come quickly. Nevertheless, as the use of empirical information for policy making has become more politically fashionable, misinformation masquerading as reality has become more dangerous. The purpose of this book has been to highlight the major sources (and consequences) of such misinformation so that policy makers cannot continue to regurgitate mistruths publicly and with impunity. We know better, and it's up to us to make sure that they do as well.

Note

1. This conclusion is consistent with the broader literature on offender decision making that was discussed in Chapter 3. In particular, if the threat of sanctions is going to influence offenders' decisions, it is most likely to do so among low-risk offenders (those targeted by the MUSTER program); this effect exists not because of the sanction threat itself, but rather because of the social costs that the imposition of the sanction may set into motion (e.g., loss of job, or shame from a spouse, friends, or family; see Pratt et al. 2006). Alternatively, higher-risk offenders (e.g., those without such social bonds) tend to be the least responsive to the kinds of sanction threats employed by the MUSTER program.

References

Alderman, J. D. 1994. Leading the public: The media's focus on crime shaped sentiment. *The Public Perspective* 513 (March/April):26–7.

Anderson, D. C. 1998. *Sensible justice: Alternatives to prison.* New York: New Press.

Andrews, D. A., and J. Bonta. 1998. *The psychology of criminal conduct.* 2nd ed. Cincinnati, OH: Anderson.

Andrews, D. A., I. Zinger, R. D. Hoge, J. Bonta, P. Gendreau, and F. T. Cullen. 1990. Does correctional treatment work? A clinically relevant and psychologically informed meta-analysis. *Criminology* 28:369–404.

Angotti, J. 1997. National survey finds crime dominates local TV news. Press release from University of Miami Office of Media and External Relations. May 6.

Anson, R., and B. Hancock. 1992. Crowding, proximity, inmate violence, and the Eighth Amendment. *Journal of Offender Rehabilitation* 17:123–32.

Applegate, B. K., F. T. Cullen, and B. S. Fisher. 1997. Public support for correctional treatment: The continuing appeal of the rehabilitative ideal. *Prison Journal* 77:237–58.

Applegate, B. K., F. T. Cullen, B. S. Fisher, and T. Van der Ven. 2000. Forgiveness and fundamentalism: Reconsidering the relationship between correctional attitudes and religion. *Criminology* 38:719–54.

Applegate, B. K., F. T. Cullen, B. G. Link, P. J. Richards, and L. Lanza-Kaduce. 1996. Determinants of public punitiveness toward drunken driving: A factorial survey approach. *Justice Quarterly* 13:57–79.

Applegate, B. K., F. T. Cullen, M. G. Turner, and J. L. Sundt. 1996. Assessing public support for three-strikes-and-you're-out laws: Global versus specific attitudes. *Crime & Delinquency* 42:517–34.

Auerhahn, K. 1999. Selective incapacitation and the problem of prediction. *Criminology* 37:703–34.

———. 2002. Selective incapacitation, three strikes, and the problem of aging prison populations: Using simulation modeling to see the future. *Criminology and Public Policy* 1:353–88.

Austin, J. 2003. Why criminology is irrelevant. *Criminology and Public Policy* 2:557–64.

Austin, J., and J. Irwin. 2001. *It's about time: America's imprisonment binge.* 3rd ed. Belmont, CA: Wadsworth.

Barzagan, M. 1994. The effects of health, environmental, and socio-psychological variables on fear of crime and its consequences among urban black elderly individuals. *International Journal of Aging and Human Development* 38:99–115.

Baum, D. 1996. *Smoke and mirrors: The war on drugs and the politics of failure.* Boston: Little, Brown.

Beccaria, C. 1764(1963). *On crimes and punishments.* Indianapolis, IN: Bobbs-Merrill.

Becker, G. S. 1968. Crime and punishment: An economic approach. *Journal of Political Economy* 76:169–217.

Beckett, K. 1997. *Making crime pay: Law and order in contemporary American politics.* New York: Oxford University Press.

Beckett, K., and T. Sasson. 2003. *The politics of injustice: Crime and punishment in America.* 2nd ed. Thousand Oaks, CA: Sage Publications.

Bellah, R. N., R. Madsen, W. M. Sullivan, A. Swindler, and S. M. Tipton. 1985. *Habits of the heart: Individualism and commitment in American life.* New York: Harper & Row.

Bennett, W. J., J. J. DiIulio, and J. P. Walters. 1996. *Body count: Moral poverty . . . and how to win America's war against crime and drugs.* New York: Simon & Schuster.

Biemer, P. P., R. M. Groves, L. E. Lyberg, N. A. Mathiowetz, and S. Sudman, eds. 1991. *Measurement errors in surveys.* New York: Wiley.

Biewen, J. 2002. Corporate-sponsored crime laws. Available at http://www.americanradioworks.org/features/corrections/html.

Blau, P. M. 1977. *Inequality and heterogeneity.* New York: Free Press.

Blau, P. M., and J. R. Blau. 1982. The cost of inequality: Metropolitan structure and violent crime. *American Sociological Review* 47:114–29.

Blumstein, A. 1982. On the racial disproportionality of United States' prison populations. *Journal of Criminal Law and Criminology* 73:1259–81.

———. 1997. Interaction of criminological research and public policy. *Journal of Quantitative Criminology* 12:349–61.

———. 2000. Disaggregating violence trends. In A. Blumstein and J. Wallman, eds. *The crime drop in America.* New York: Cambridge University Press.

Blumstein, A., and A. Beck. 1999. Population growth in U.S. prisons. In *Prisons,* ed. M. Tonry and J. Petersilia, 17–62. Chicago: University of Chicago Press.

Blumstein, A., and J. Cohen. 1973. A theory of the stability of punishment. *Journal of Criminal Law and Criminology* 64:198–206.

Blumstein, A., J. Cohen, and D. P. Farrington. 1988. Criminal career research: Its value for criminology. *Criminology* 26:1–35.

Blumstein, A., J. Cohen, S. E. Martin, and M. H. Tonry. 1983. *Research on sentencing: The search for reform.* Washington, DC: National Academy Press.

Blumstein, A., J. Cohen, J. Roth, and C. Visher. 1986. *Criminal careers and "career criminals."* Panel on Research on Criminal Careers. National Research Council. Washington, DC: National Academy Press.

Blumstein, A. J., and R. Rosenfeld. 1998. Exploring recent trends in U.S. homicide rates. *Journal of Criminal Law and Criminology* 88:1175–216.

Blumstein, A. J., and J. Wallman. 2000. *The crime drop in America.* New York: Cambridge University Press.

Bobrow, D. S., and J. S. Dryzek. 1987. *Policy analysis by design.* Pittsburgh, PA: University of Pittsburgh Press.

Bonderman, J. 2001. *Working with victims of gun violence. Office for Victims of Crime (OVC) Bulletin*, July. Washington, DC: United States Department of Justice.

Bowker, L. 1980. *Prison victimization.* New York: Elsevier.

Braun, S., and J. Pasternak. 1994. A nation with peril on its mind. *Los Angeles Times*, February 19:A1, A16.

Brooks, K., V. Schiraldi, and J. Ziedenberg. 2000. *School house hype: Two years later.* Washington, DC: Justice Policy Institute/Children's Law Center.

Brown, M. P., and P. Elrod. 1995. Electronic house arrest: An examination of citizen attitudes. *Crime & Delinquency* 41:332–46.

Bureau of Justice Statistics. 1998. *Prison and jail inmates at midyear 1997.* Washington, DC: U.S. Department of Justice.

———. 1999. *Felony sentences in state courts, 1996.* Washington, DC: Government Printing Office.

———. 2001. *Probation and parole statistics.* Washington, DC: U.S. Department of Justice.

———. 2005. *Substance dependence, abuse, and treatment of jail inmates, 2002.* Washington, DC: U.S. Department of Justice.

———. 2006a. *Prisoners in 2006.* Washington, DC: U.S. Department of Justice.

———. 2006b. *Drug use and dependence: State and federal prisoners, 2004.* Washington, DC: U.S. Department of Justice.

———. 2007a. *Expenditure and employment statistics.* Washington, DC: U.S. Department of Justice.

———. 2007b. *Reentry trends in the United States.* Washington, DC: U.S. Department of Justice.

Bursik, R. J. 1988. Social disorganization and theories of crime and delinquency: Problems and prospects. *Criminology* 26:519–51.

Bursik, R. J., and H. G. Grasmick. 1993. Economic deprivation and neighborhood crime rates, 1960–1980. *Law and Society Review* 27:263–83.

Butts, J. A., and D. P. Mears. 2001. Reviving juvenile justice in a get-tough era. *Youth and Society* 33:169–98.

Byrne, J. M., A. J. Lurigio, and J. Petersilia, eds. 1992. *Smart sentencing: The emergence of intermediate sanctions.* Newbury Park, CA: Sage Publications.

Camp, S. D., G. G. Gaes, N. P. Langan, and W. G. Saylor. 2003. The influence of prisons on inmate misconduct: A multilevel investigation. *Justice Quarterly* 20:501–33.

Caplan, G. 1973. Reflections on the nationalization of crime, 1964–1968. *Law and the Social Order* 5(3).

Chaiken, M. R., and J. Chaiken. 1984. Offender types and public policy. *Crime & Delinquency* 30:195–226.

Chambliss, W. J. 1999. *Power, politics, and crime.* Boulder, CO: Westview Press.

Chase-Lansdale, P. L., R. A. Gordon, J. Brooks-Gunn, and P. K. Klebanov. 1997. Neighborhood and family influences on the intellectual and behavioral competence of preschool and early school-aged children. In *Neighborhood poverty: Volume 1. Context and consequences for children,* ed. J. Brooks-Gunn, G. J. Duncan, and J. L. Aber. New York: Russell Sage Foundation.

Cheung, A. 2002. *Prison privatization and the use of incarceration.* Washington, DC: The Sentencing Project.

Chiricos, T., S. Eschholz, and M. Gertz. 1997. Crime, news, and fear of crime: Toward an identification of audience effects. *Social Problems* 44:342–57.

Chiricos, T., K. Padgett, and M. Gertz. 2000. Fear, TV news, and the reality of crime. *Criminology* 38:755–86.

Clarke, R. V. 1995. Situational crime prevention. In *Building a safer society: Strategic approaches to crime prevention,* ed. M. Tonry and D. P. Farrington, 91–150. New York: Cambridge University Press.

Clarke, R. V., and D. Cornish. 2001. Rational choice. In *Explaining criminals and crime: Essays in contemporary criminological theory,* ed. R. Paternoster and R. Bachman, 23–42. Los Angeles: Roxbury.

Clear, T. R. 1994. *Harm in American penology.* Albany: State University of New York Press.

Clear, T. R., G. F. Cole, and M. D. Reisig. 2006. *American corrections.* 7th ed. Belmont, CA: Wadsworth/Thomson.

Clear, T. R., D. R. Rose, and J. A. Ryder. 2001. Incarceration and the community: The problem of removing and returning offenders. *Crime & Delinquency* 47:335–51.

Clear, T. R., D. R. Rose, E. Waring, and K. Scully. 2003. Coercive mobility and crime: A preliminary examination of concentrated incarceration and social disorganization. *Justice Quarterly* 20:33–63.

Cochran, J. K., M. B. Chamlin, and M. Seth. 1994. Deterrence or brutalization? An impact assessment of Oklahoma's return to capital punishment. *Criminology* 32:107–34.

Cohen, J. 1983. Incapacitation as a strategy for crime control: Possibilities and pitfalls. In vol. 2 of *Crime and justice: An annual review of research,* ed. M. Tonry and N. Morris. Chicago: University of Chicago Press.

———. 1986. Research on criminal careers: Individual frequency rates and offense seriousness. In vol. 1 of *Criminal careers and "career criminals,"* ed. A. Blumstein, J. Cohen, J. Roth, and C. Visher. Washington, DC: National Academy Press.

Cohen, L. E., and M. Felson. 1979. Social change and crime rate trends: A routine activities approach. *American Sociological Review* 44:588–608.

Cohen, M. A., R. T. Rust, and S. Steen. 2006. Prevention, crime control, or cash? Public preferences towards criminal justice spending priorities. *Justice Quarterly* 23:317–35.

Cohen, R. E. 1992. *Washington at work: Back rooms and clean air.* New York: Macmillan.

Coleman, J. S. 1988. Social capital and the creation of human capital. *American Journal of Sociology* 94 Supplement:S95–S120.

———. 1990. *Foundations of social theory.* Cambridge, MA: Harvard University Press.

Colson, C. 1989. Alternatives to reduce prison crowding. *Journal of State Government* 62:59–94.

Colvin, M. 1992. *The penitentiary in crisis.* Albany: State University of New York Press.

Conklin, J. E. 2003. *Why crime rates fell.* Boston: Allyn & Bacon.

Conrad, J. 1973. Corrections and simple justice. *Journal of Criminal Law, Criminology, and Police Science* 64:208–17.

Cornish, D., and R. V. Clarke. 1986. *The reasoning criminal: Rational choice perspectives on offending.* New York: Springer.

Cressey, D. R. 1978. Criminological theory, social science, and the repression of crime. *Criminology* 16:171–91.

Cronin, T. E., T. Z. Cronin, and M. E. Milakovich. 1981. *U.S. vs. crime in the streets.* Bloomington: Indiana University Press.

Cullen, F. T. 1994. Social support as an organizing concept for criminology: Presidential address to the Academy of Criminal Justice Sciences. *Justice Quarterly* 11:527–59.

———. 2005. The twelve people who saved rehabilitation: How the science of criminology made a difference. *Criminology* 43:1–42.

Cullen, F. T., J. B. Cullen, and J. F. Wozniak. 1988. Is rehabilitation dead? The myth of the punitive public. *Journal of Criminal Justice* 16:303–17.

Cullen, F. T., B. S. Fisher, and B. K. Applegate. 2000. Public opinion about punishment and corrections. In vol. 27 of *Crime and justice: A review of research,* ed. M. Tonry. Chicago: University of Chicago Press.

Cullen, F. T., and P. Gendreau. 1989. The effectiveness of correctional rehabilitation: Reconsidering the "nothing works" debate. In *The American prison: Issues in research and policy,* ed. L. Goodstein and D. MacKenzie. New York: Plenum.

———. 2000. Assessing correctional rehabilitation: Policy, practice, and prospects. In vol. 3 of *Criminal justice 2000,* ed. J. Horney. Washington, DC: National Institute of Justice.

Cullen, F. T., and K. E. Gilbert. 1982. *Reaffirming rehabilitation.* Cincinnati, OH: Anderson.

Cullen, F. T., K. M. Golden, and J. B. Cullen. 1983. Is child saving dead? Attitudes toward juvenile rehabilitation in Illinois. *Journal of Criminal Justice* 11:1–13.

Cullen, F. T., T. C. Pratt, S. L. Miceli, and M. M. Moon. 2002. Dangerous liaison? Rational choice theory as the basis for correctional intervention. In *Rational choice and criminal behavior: Recent research and future challenges,* ed. A. R. Piquero and S. G. Tibbetts. New York: Routledge.

Cullen, F. T., J. P. Wright, and B. K. Applegate. 1996. Control in the community: The limits of reform? In *Choosing correctional options that work: Defining the demand and evaluating the supply,* ed. A. T. Harland, 69–116. Thousand Oaks, CA: Sage Publications.

Cullen, F. T., J. P. Wright, S. Brown, M. M. Moon, M. B. Blankenship, and B. K. Applegate. 1998. Public support for early intervention programs: Implications for a progressive policy agenda. *Crime & Delinquency* 44:187–204.

Cullen, F. T., J. P. Wright, and M. B. Chamlin. 1999. Social support and social reform: A progressive crime control agenda. *Crime & Delinquency* 45:188–207.

Currie, E. 1998. *Crime and punishment in America.* New York: Henry Holt.

———. 1999. Reflections on crime and criminology at the millennium. *Western Criminology Review* 2(1). Available online at http:www.wcr.sonoma.edu.

Decker, S. H., and B. van Winkle. 1996. *Life in the gang: Family, friends, and violence.* New York: Cambridge University Press.

DeFronzo, J. 1996. Welfare and burglary. *Crime & Delinquency* 42:233–30.

———. 1997. Welfare and homicide. *Journal of Research in Crime and Delinquency* 34:395–406.

Delisi, M. 2005. *Career criminals in society.* Thousand Oaks, CA: Sage Publications.

DiIulio, J. J. 1987. *Governing prisons: A comparative study of correctional management.* New York: Free Press.

———. 1988. What's wrong with private prisons? *Public Interest* 29:66–83.

———. 1991. *No escape: The future of American corrections.* New York: Basic Books.

———. 1994. Let 'em rot. *The Wall Street Journal.* January 26:A-14.

———. 1995. Arresting ideas. *Policy Review* 74(Fall):15.

———. 1997. Are voters fools? Crime, public opinion, and representative democracy. *Corrections Management Quarterly* 1(3):1–5.

———. 1999. Two million prisoners are enough. *The Wall Street Journal.* March 12.

DiIulio, J. J., and A. M. Piehl. 1991. Does prison pay? The stormy national debate over the cost-effectiveness of imprisonment. *Brookings Review* (Fall):28–35.

Dobash, R., R. Dobash, and S. Gutteridge. 1986. *The imprisonment of women.* Oxford, UK: Blackwell.

Doble, J., S. Immerwahr, and A. Richardson. 1991. *Punishing criminals: The people of Delaware consider the options.* New York: Edna McConnell Clark Foundation.

Doble, J., and J. Klein. 1989. *Punishing criminals: The public's view, an Alabama survey.* New York: Edna McConnell Clark Foundation.

Doble Research Associates. 1995a. *Crime and corrections: The views of the people of North Carolina.* Englewood Cliffs, NJ: Author.

———. 1995b. *Crime and corrections: The views of the people of Oklahoma.* Englewood Cliffs, NJ: Author.

———. 1995c. *Crime and corrections: The views of the people of Oregon.* Englewood Cliffs, NJ: Author.

Doleschal, E., and N. Klamputs. 1973. Toward a new criminology. *Crime & Delinquency Literature* 5:607–27.

Donohue, J. J. 1998. Understanding the time path of crime. *Journal of Criminal Law and Criminology* 88:1423–51.

Donohue, W. A. 1985. *The politics of the American Civil Liberties Union.* New Brunswick, NJ: Transaction.

Donziger, S. R. 1996. *The real war on crime: The report of the National Criminal Justice Commission.* New York: Harper Collins.

Dowden, C., and D. A. Andrews. 1999. What works for female offenders: A meta-analytic review. *Crime & Delinquency* 45(4):438–52.

———. 2000. Effective correctional treatment and violent reoffending: A meta-analysis. *Canadian Journal of Criminology* 42(4): 449–67.

———. 2004. The importance of staff practice in delivering effective correctional treatment: A meta-analytic review of core correctional practice. *International Journal of Offender Therapy and Comparative Criminology* 48:203–14.

Dumond, R. W. 2000. Inmate sexual assault: The plague that still persists. *The Prison Journal* 80:407–14.

———. 2003. Confronting America's most ignored crime problem: The prison rape elimination act of 2003. *The Journal of the American Academy of Psychiatry and the Law* 31:354–60.

Dworkin, R. 1985. *A matter of principle.* Cambridge, MA: Harvard University Press.

Eichenthal, D., and J. Jacobs. 1991. Enforcing the criminal law in state prisons. *Justice Quarterly* 8:238–303.

Eisenstein, J., and H. Jacob. 1977. *Felony justice.* Boston: Little, Brown.

Ekirch, R. A. 1987. *Bound for America: The transportation of British convicts to the colonies, 1717–1785.* Oxford, UK: Clarendon Press.

Elrod, P., and M. P. Brown. 1996. Predicting public support for electronic house arrest: Results from a New York county survey. *American Behavioral Scientist* 39:461–73.

Eschholz, S. 1997. The media and fear of crime: A survey of the research. *Journal of Law and Public Policy* 9:37–59.

Eskridge, C. W. 2005. The state of the field of criminology. *Journal of Contemporary Criminal Justice* 21:296–308.

Fagan, J., and F. E. Zimring, eds. 2000. *The changing borders of juvenile justice.* Chicago: University of Chicago Press.

Fairbank, Maslin, Maullin, and Associates. 1997. *Resources for Youth California survey.* Santa Monica, CA: Author.

Farkas, S. 1993. Pennsylvanians prefer alternatives to prison. *Overcrowded Times* 4(2):1, 13–15.

Farrington, D. P. 1986. Age and crime. In vol. 7 of *Crime and justice: A review of research,* ed. M. Tonry and N. Morris. Chicago: University of Chicago Press.

———. 1989. Self-reported and official offending from adolescence through adulthood. In *Cross-national research in self-reported crime and delinquency,* ed. M. W. Klein. Boston: Kluwer Academic.

———. 1994. Early developmental prevention of juvenile delinquency. *Criminal Behaviour and Mental Health* 4:209–27.

Fass, S. M., and C. Pi. 2002. Getting tough on juvenile crime: An analysis of costs and benefits. *Crime & Delinquency* 39:363–99.

Feeley, M. 2002. Entrepreneurs of punishment: The legacy of privatization. *Punishment and Society* 4:321–44.

Feeley, M., and E. Rubin. 1998. *Judicial policy making and the modern state: How the courts reformed America's prisons.* New York: Cambridge University Press.

Feeley, M., and J. Simon. 1992. The new penology: Notes on the emerging strategy of corrections and its implications. *Criminology* 30:449–71.

Feinman, C. 1986. *Women in the criminal justice system.* New York: Praeger.

Feld, B. C. 1998. Juvenile and criminal justice systems' responses to youth violence. In vol. 24 of *Crime and justice: A review of research,* ed. M. Tonry. Chicago: University of Chicago Press.

Felson, M. 2002. *Crime and everyday life: Insights and implications for society.* 2nd ed. Thousand Oaks, CA: Pine Forge Press.

Felson, M., and L. E. Cohen. 1980. Human ecology and crime: A routine activities approach. *Human Ecology* 8:389–406.

Fishman, L. T. 1990. *Women at the wall: A study of prisoners' wives doing time on the outside.* Albany: State University of New York Press.

Flanagan, T. J. 1996. Reform or punish: Americans' views of the correctional system. In *Americans view crime and justice: A national public survey,* ed. T. J. Flanagan and D. R. Longmire. Thousand Oaks, CA: Sage Publications.

Foley, H. A., C. O. Carlton, and R. J. Howell. 1996. The relationship of attention deficit hyperactivity disorder and conduct disorder to juvenile delinquency: Legal implications. *Bulletin of the American Academy of Psychiatry Law* 24:333–45.

Foucalt, M. 1977. *Discipline and punish: The birth of the prison.* New York: Vintage.

Fox, J. A. 2000. Demographics and U.S. homicide. In *The crime drop in America,* ed. A. Blumstein and J. Wallman. New York: Cambridge University Press.

Franz, M. M., P. Freedman, K. M. Goldstein, and T. N. Ridout. 2007. *Campaign advertising and American democracy.* Philadelphia: Temple University Press.

Freedman, E. 1974. Their sisters' keepers: An historical perspective on female correctional institutions in the United States. *Feminist Studies* 2:78–95.

Friedman, L. M. 1993. *Crime and punishment in American history.* New York: Basic Books.

Friedman, W. 1998. Volunteerism and the decline of violent crime. *Journal of Criminal Law and Criminology* 88:1453–74.

Fulton, B., E. J. Latessa, A. Stichman, and L. F. Travis. 1997. The state of ISP: Research and policy implications. *Federal Probation* 61(4):65–75.

Furstenburg, F. F. 1993. How families manage risk and opportunity in dangerous neighborhoods. In *Sociology and the public agenda,* ed. W. J. Wilson, 231–58. Newbury Park, CA: Sage Publications.

Gaes, G., and W. McGuire. 1985. Prison violence: The contribution of crowding versus other determinants of prison assault rates. *Journal of Research in Crime & Delinquency* 22:41–65.

Galbraith, J. K. 1996. *The good society: The humane agenda.* New York: Houghton Mifflin.

Gallup, G. 1999. *Gallup social and economic indicators.* Princeton, NJ: Gallup Poll (February).

Gallup Poll. 2007. *Perceptions of Crime Problem Remain Curiously Negative.* (October). Gallup, Inc.

Garland, D. 1990. *Punishment and modern society: A study in social theory.* Chicago: University of Chicago Press.

Gau, J. M., and T. C. Pratt. Forthcoming. Broken windows or window dressing? Citizens' (in)ability to tell the difference between disorder and crime. *Criminology and Public Policy.*

Geis, G., A. Mobley, and D. Shichor. 1999. Private prisons, criminological research, and conflict of interest: A case study. *Crime & Delinquency* 45:372–88.

Gendreau, P. 1996. The principles of effective intervention with offenders. In *Choosing correctional options that work,* ed. A. T. Harland, 117–30. Thousand Oaks, CA: Sage Publications.

Gendreau, P., and R. R. Ross. 1987. Revivification of rehabilitation: Evidence from the 1980s. *Justice Quarterly,* 4:349.

Gensheimer, L. K., J. P. Mayer, R. Gottschalk, and W. S. Davidson. 1986. Diverting youth from the juvenile justice system: A meta-analysis of intervention efficacy. In *Youth violence,* ed. S. J. Apter and A. P. Goldstein, 39–57. New York: Pergamon.

Gest, T. 2001. *Crime and politics: Big government's erratic campaign for law and order.* New York: Oxford University Press.

Gido, R. L. 2002. Inmates with HIV/AIDS: A growing concern. In *Prison sex: Practice and policy,* ed. C. Hensley, 101–10. London: Lynne Rienner.

Gilsinan, J. F. 1991. Public policy and criminology: A historical and philosophical reassessment. *Justice Quarterly* 8:201–6.

Goddard, H. H. 1914. *Feeble-mindedness.* New York: MacMillan.

Goldkamp, J. S., M. D. White, and J. B. Robinson. 2001. Do drug courts work? Getting inside the drug court black box. *Journal of Drug Issues* 31:27–72.

Goodstein, L., and J. Hepburn. 1985. *Determinate sentencing and imprisonment: A failure of reform.* Cincinnati, OH: Anderson.

Gordon, D. R. 1990. *The justice juggernaut.* New Brunswick, NJ: Rutgers University Press.

Gottfredson, M. R. 1982. The social scientist and rehabilitative crime policy. *Criminology* 20:29–42.

Gottfredson, M. R., and T. Hirschi. 1990. *A general theory of crime.* Palo Alto, CA: Stanford University Press.

Gottschalk, R., W. S. Davidson, J. Mayer, and L. K. Genshemier. 1987. Behavioral approaches with juvenile offenders: A meta-analysis of long-term treatment efficacy. In *Behavioral approaches to crime and delinquency: A handbook,* ed. E. K. Morris and C. J. Brackman, 399–422. New York: Plenum.

Graber, D. A. 1993. *Mass media and American politics.* 4th ed. Washington, DC: CQ Press.

Greenberg, D. 1975. The incapacitative effect of imprisonment: Some estimates. *Law and Society Review* 9:541–80.

Greenberg, D. F., R. C. Kessler, and C. H. Logan. 1979. A panel model of crime rates and arrest rates. *American Sociological Review* 44:843–50.

Greenwood, P. W., and A. Abrahamse. 1982. *Selective incapacitation.* Santa Monica, CA: Rand.

Griset, P. L. 1991. *Determinate sentencing: The promise and the reality of retributive justice.* Albany: State University of New York Press.

Grissmer, D., A. Flanagan, and S. Williamson. 1998. Why did the black–white score gap narrow in the 1970s and 1980s? In *The black–white test score gap,* ed. C. Jencks and M. Phillips. Washington, DC: The Brookings Institution.

Grogger, J. 2000. An economic model of recent trends in violence. In *The crime drop in America,* ed. A. Blumstein and J. Wallman, 266–87. Cambridge, UK: Cambridge University Press.

Guryan, J. 2001. *Desegregation and black dropout rates.* Working paper 8345. Cambridge, MA: National Bureau of Economic Research.

Gusfield, J. 1981. *The culture of public problems: Drinking, driving, and the symbolic order.* Chicago: University of Chicago Press.

Hagan, J. 1994. *Crime and disrepute.* Thousand Oaks, CA: Pine Forge Press.

Hale, C. 1996. Fear of crime: A review of the literature. *International Review of Victimology* 4:79–150.

Hallett, M. 2002. Race, crime and for-profit imprisonment: Social disorganization as market opportunity. *Punishment and Society* 4:369–93.

Hallinan, J. T. 2001. *Going up the river: Travels in a prison nation.* New York: Random House.

Hamilton, Z. K., C. J. Sullivan, B. M. Veysey, and M. Grillo. 2006. Diverting multi-problem youth from juvenile justice: Investigating the importance of community influence on placement and recidivism. *Behavioral Sciences and the Law* 24:1–22.

Harcourt, B. E. 2001. *Illusion of order: The false promise of broken windows policing.* Cambridge, MA: Harvard University Press.

Harer, M., and D. Steffensmeier. 1996. Race and prison violence. *Criminology* 34:323–55.

Hargrove, T. 2001. Number of home-schooled kids rises as school shootings climb. *Houston Chronicle.* April 6.

Harlow, R. E., J. M. Darley, and P. H. Robinson. 1995. The severity of intermediate penal sanctions: A psychophysical scaling approach for obtaining community perceptions. *Journal of Quantitative Criminology* 11:71–95.

Harris, L. 1968. Changing public attitudes toward crime and corrections. *Federal Probation* 32(4):9–16.

Hassine, V. 1999. *Life without parole.* Los Angeles: Roxbury.

Hay, C. 2001. Parenting, self-control, and delinquency: A test of self-control theory. *Criminology* 39:707–36.

Heath, L., and K. Gilbert. 1996. Mass media and fear of crime. *American Behavioral Scientist* 39:379–86.

Hensley, C., R. Tewksbury, and T. Castle. 2003. Characteristics of prison sexual assault targets in male Oklahoma correctional facilities. *Journal of Interpersonal Violence* 18:595–606.

Herrnstein, R. J., and C. Murray. 1994. *The bell curve: Intelligence and class structure in American life.* New York: Free Press.

Hirsch, A. J. 1992. *The rise of the penitentiary.* New Haven, CT: Yale University Press.

Histed, A. T. 2003. *A socio-historical analysis of the Michigan Youth Correctional Facility: Economic turmoil as an impetus for social and political change.* Unpublished master's thesis, Michigan State University.

Holtfreter, K., M. D. Reisig, and M. Morash. 2004. Poverty, state capital, and recidivism among women offenders. *Criminology and Public Policy* 3:185–208.

Hooks, G., C. Mosher, T. Rotolo, and L. Labao. 2004. The prison industry: Carceral expansion and employment in U.S. counties, 1969–1994. *Social Science Quarterly* 85:37–57.

Hough, M., and J. V. Roberts. 1999. Sentencing trends in Britain: Public knowledge and public opinion. *Punishment and Society* 1:11–26.

Howell, J. C., and J. D. Hawkins. 1998. Prevention of youth violence. In vol. 24 of *Crime and justice: A review of research,* ed. M. Tonry. Chicago: University of Chicago Press.

Huntington, N., D. J. Moses, and B. M. Veysey. 2005. Developing and implementing a comprehensive approach to serving women with co-occurring disorders and histories of violence. *Journal of Community Psychology* 33:395–410.

Hutto, T. D. 1988. Corrections partnership: The public and private sectors work together. *Corrections Today* 50:20–2.

Izzo, R., and R. R. Ross. 1990. Meta-analysis of rehabilitation programs for juvenile delinquents. *Criminal Justice and Behavior* 17:134–42.

Jacobs, G. 1993. *Punishing criminals: Pennsylvanians consider the options.* New York: Public Agenda Foundation.

Jacobs, J. 1977. *Stateville: The penitentiary in mass society.* Chicago: University of Chicago Press.

Jacoby, J. E., and F. T. Cullen. 1998. The structure of punishment norms: Applying the Rossi-Berk model. *Journal of Criminal Law and Criminology* 89:245–312.

Jencks, C., and M. Phillips. 1998. The black–white test score gap: An introduction. In *The black–white test score gap*, ed. C. Jencks and M. Phillips. Washington, DC: The Brookings Institution.

Johnson, A. G. 2006. *Privilege, power, and difference*. 2nd ed. New York: McGraw-Hill.

Johnson, B., A. Golub, and E. Dunlap. 2000. The rise and decline of hard drugs, drug markets, and violence in inner-city New York. In *The crime drop in America*, ed. A. Blumstein and J. Wallman, 164–206. Cambridge, UK: Cambridge University Press.

Johnson, R. 1990. *Death work: A study of the modern execution process*. Pacific Grove, CA: Brooks/Cole.

Jones, T. R., and T. C. Pratt. 2008. The prevalence of sexual violence in prison: The state of the knowledge base and implications for evidence-based correctional policymaking. *International Journal of Offender Therapy and Comparative Criminology* 52:280–95.

Keil, T. J., and G. F. Vito. 1991. Fear of crime and attitudes toward capital punishment: A structural equations model. *Justice Quarterly* 8:447–64.

Ketcham, K., and W. F. Asbury. 2000. *Beyond the influence: Understanding and defeating alcoholism*. New York: Bantam.

Kinder, D. R. 1998. Opinion and action in the realm of politics. In vol. 2 of *The handbook of social psychology*, ed. D. T. Gilbert, S. T. Fiske, and G. Lindzey, 4th ed. Boston: McGraw-Hill.

Kingdon, J. 1995. *Agendas, alternatives, and public policies*. 2nd ed. New York: Harper Collins.

Klite, P., R. A. Bardwell, and J. Salzman. 1997. *Baaad news: Local TV news in America*. Denver, CO: Rocky Mountain Media Watch.

Knott, J., and G. Miller. 1987. *Reforming bureaucracy: The politics of institutional choice*. Englewood Cliffs, NJ: Prentice Hall.

Knowles, G. J. 1999. Male prison rape: A search for causation and prevention. *The Howard Journal* 38:267–82.

Kozol, J. 2005. *The shame of the nation: The restoration of apartheid schooling in America*. New York: Crown.

Kristof, N. 1996. In Japan, nothing to fear but fear itself. *New York Times*. May 19, Section 4, p. 4.

Kubrin, C. E., and E. A. Stewart. 2006. Predicting who reoffends: The neglected role of neighborhood context in recidivism studies. *Criminology* 44:165–98.

Kunselman, J., R. Tewksbury, R. W. Dumond, and D. A. Dumond. 2002. Nonconsensual sexual behavior. In *Prison sex: Practice and policy*, ed. C. Hensley, 27–49. London: Lynne Rienner.

Kupchik, A. 2003. Prosecuting adolescents in criminal court: Criminal or juvenile justice? *Social Problems* 50:439–60.

Kupers, T. A. 1996. Trauma and its sequelae in male prisons: Effects of confinement, overcrowding, and diminished services. *American Journal of Orthopsychiatry* 66:189–96.

Kurki, L., and N. Morris. 2001. The purpose, practice, and problem of supermax prisons. In vol. 28 of *Crime and justice: An annual review of research,* ed. N. Morris and M. Tonry, 385–424. Chicago: University of Chicago Press.

Kury, H., and U. Smartt. 2002. Prisoner-on-prisoner violence: Victimization of young offenders in prison. Some German findings. *Criminal Justice* 2:411–37.

Lab, S. P, M. R. Williams, J. E. Holcomb, M. W. Burek, W. R. King, and M. E. Buerger. 2008. *Criminal justice: The essentials.* New York: Oxford University Press.

LaFree, G. 1998. Social institutions and the crime "bust" of the 1990s. *Journal of Criminal Law and Criminology* 88:1325–68.

LaFree, G., and R. Arum. 2006. The impact of racially inclusive schooling on adult incarceration rates among U.S. cohorts of African Americans and whites since 1930. *Criminology* 44:73–104.

LaFree, G., and K. A. Drass. 2002. Counting crime booms among nations: Evidence for homicide victimization rates, 1956 to 1998. *Criminology* 40:769–800.

Land, K. C., D. Cantor, and S. T. Russell. 1995. Unemployment and crime rate fluctuations in the post–World War II United States. In *Crime and inequality,* ed. J. Hagan and R. D. Peterson. Stanford, CA: Stanford University Press.

Langan, P. A., and J. M. Brown. 1997. *Felony sentences in state courts, 1994.* Washington, DC: Bureau of Justice Statistics.

Langan, P. A., and H. Graziadei. 1995. *Felony sentences in state courts, 1992.* Washington, DC: Bureau of Justice Statistics.

Langan, P. A., and D. Levin. 2002. *Recidivism of prisoners released in 1994.* Washington, DC: Bureau of Justice Statistics.

Langan, P. A., C. Perkins, and J. M. Chaiken. 1995. *Felony sentences in the United States, 1990.* Washington, DC: Bureau of Justice Statistics.

Latessa, E. J., and H. E. Allen. 2003. *Corrections in the community.* 3rd ed. Cincinnati, OH: Anderson.

Laub, J. H., and R. J. Sampson. 2003. *Shared beginnings, divergent lives.* Cambridge, MA: Harvard University Press.

Lemert, E. 1967. The juvenile court: Questions and realities. In *The President's Commission of Law Enforcement and the Administration of Justice, Task Force Report: Juvenile Delinquency and Youth Crime.* Washington, DC: Government Printing Office.

Levitt, S. D., and S. J. Dubner. 2005. *Freakonomics.* New York: Harper Collins.

Levrant, S., F. T. Cullen, B. Fulton, and J. F. Wozniak. 1999. Reconsidering restorative justice: The corruption of benevolence revisited? *Crime & Delinquency* 45:3–27.

Lewis, D. A., and G. Salem. 1986. *Fear of crime: Incivility and the production of a social problem.* New Brunswick, NJ: Transaction.

Lewiston Morning Tribune. 2003. Opinion page. May 24, 12A.

Lilly, J. R., F. T. Cullen, and R. A. Ball. 2007. *Criminological theory: Context and consequences*. 3rd ed. Thousand Oaks, CA: Sage Publications.

Lilly, J. R., and M. Deflem. 1996. Profit and reality: An examination of the corrections-commercial complex. *Crime & Delinquency* 42:3–20.

Lilly, J. R., and P. Knepper. 1993. The corrections-commercial complex. *Crime & Delinquency* 39:150–66.

Lipsey, M. 1992. Juvenile delinquency treatment: A meta-analytic inquiry into the variability of effects. In *Meta-analysis for explanation*, ed. T. D. Cook et al., 83–127. New York: Russell Sage Foundation.

———. 1995. What do we learn from 400 studies on the effectiveness of treatment with juvenile delinquents? *What works: Reducing reoffending*, ed. J. McGuire, 63–78. Chichester, UK: Wiley.

Lipton, D. S., R. Martinson, and J. Wilks. 1975. *The effectiveness of correctional treatment: A survey of treatment evaluation studies*. New York: Praeger.

Lockwood, D. 1980. *Prison sexual violence*. New York: Elsevier.

Logan, C. H. 1975. Arrest rates and deterrence. *Social Science Quarterly* 56:376–89.

———. 1990. *Private prisons: Cons and pros*. New York: Oxford University Press.

Lombroso-Ferrero, G. 1911. *Criminal man, according to the classification of Cesare Lombroso*. New York: Putnam.

Longmire, D. R. 1996. Americans' attitudes about the ultimate weapon: Capital punishment. In *Americans view crime and justice: A national public opinion survey*, ed. T. J. Flanagan and D. R. Longmire. Thousand Oaks, CA: Sage Publications.

Losel, F., and P. Koferl. 1989. Evaluation research on correctional treatment in West Germany: A meta-analysis. In *Criminal behavior and the justice system: Psychological perspectives*, ed. H. Wegener et al., 334–55. New York: Springer-Verlag.

Lott, J. R. 2000. *More guns, less crime: Understanding crime and gun control laws*. Chicago: University of Chicago Press.

Lowenkamp, C. T., F. T. Cullen, and T. C. Pratt. 2003. Replicating Sampson and Groves's test of social disorganization theory: Revisiting a criminological classic. *Journal of Research in Crime and Delinquency* 40:351–73.

Lutze, F. E. 1998. Are shock incarceration programs more rehabilitative than traditional prison? A survey of inmates. *Justice Quarterly* 15:547–63.

Lynch, J. P., and W. J. Sabol. 2000. Prison use and social control. In vol. 3 of *Criminal justice 2000: Policies, processes, and decisions of the criminal justice system*, ed. J. Horney, 7–44. Washington, DC: U.S. Department of Justice, National Institute of Justice.

MacKenzie, D. 2000. Evidence-based corrections: Identifying what works. *Crime & Delinquency* 46:457–71.

———. 2001. Corrections and sentencing in the 21st century: Evidence-based corrections and sentencing. *The Prison Journal* 81:299–312.

Maguire, K., and A. L. Pastore. 1995. *Sourcebook of criminal justice statistics, 1995.* Washington, DC: U.S. Department of Justice, Bureau of Justice Statistics.

———. 1997. *Sourcebook of criminal justice statistics, 1997.* Washington, DC: U.S. Department of Justice, Bureau of Justice Statistics.

———. 1998. *Sourcebook of criminal justice statistics, 1998.* Washington, DC: U.S. Department of Justice, Bureau of Justice Statistics.

Mann, C. D., and J. P. Cronan. 2001. Forecasting sexual abuse in prison: The prison subculture of masculinity as a backdrop for "deliberate indifference." *Journal of Criminal Law and Criminology* 92:127–86.

Mann, C. R. 1993. *Unequal justice.* Bloomington: Indiana University Press.

Manza, J., C. Brooks, and C. Uggen. 2004. Public attitudes toward felon disenfranchisement in the United States. *Public Opinion Quarterly* 68:275–86.

Manza, J., and C. Uggen. 2004. Punishment and democracy: Disenfranchisement of nonincarcerated felons in the United States. *Perspectives on Politics* 2:491–505.

Marenin, O. 1995. The state of plea bargaining in Alaska. *Journal of Crime and Justice* 18:167–97.

Mariner, J. 2001. *No escape: Male rape in U.S. prisons.* USA: Human Rights Watch.

Martinson, R. 1974. What works? Questions and answers about prison reform. *The Public Interest* (Spring):22–54.

———. 1979. New findings, new views: A note of caution regarding sentencing reform. *Hofstra Law Review* 7:243–58.

Maruna, S. 2001. *Making good: How ex-convicts reform and rebuild their lives.* Washington, DC: American Psychological Association.

Marvell, T. B., and C. E. Moody. 1996. Specification problems, police levels, and crime rates. *Criminology* 34:609–46.

Mauer, M. 1999. *Race to incarcerate.* New York: The New Press.

Mauer, M., and T. Huling. 1995. *Young black Americans and the criminal justice system.* Washington, DC: The Sentencing Project.

Mayer, J. P., L. K. Gensheimer, W. S. Davidson, and R. Gottschalk. 1986. Social learning treatment within juvenile justice: A meta-analysis of impact in the natural environment. In *Youth violence,* ed. S. J. Apter and A. P. Goldstein. New York: Pergamon.

Mazerolle, L. G., C. Kadleck, and J. Roehl. 1998. Controlling drug and disorder problems: The role of place managers. *Criminology* 36:371–404.

McCain, G., V. Cox, and P. Paulus. 1980. *The effect of prison crowding on inmate behavior.* Washington, DC: National Institute of Justice.

McCorkle, R. C. 1993. Fear of victimization and symptoms of psychopathology among prison inmates. *Journal of Offender Rehabilitation* 19:27–41.

McDonald, L. 1976. *The sociology of law and order*. Boulder, CO: Westview Press.

McDowall, D., C. Loftin, and B. Wiersema. 1992. A comparative study of the preventive effects of mandatory sentencing laws for gun crimes. *Journal of Criminal Law and Criminology* 83:378–94.

McGloin, J. M., and T. C. Pratt. 2003. Cognitive ability and delinquent behavior among inner-city youth: A life-course analysis of main, mediating, and interaction effects. *International Journal of Offender Therapy and Comparative Criminology* 47:253–71.

McGloin, J. M., T. C. Pratt, and J. Maahs. 2004. Re-thinking the IQ-delinquency relationship: A longitudinal analysis of multiple theoretical models. *Justice Quarterly* 21:601–31.

McGloin, J. M., T. C. Pratt, and A. R. Piquero. 2006. A life-course analysis of the criminogenic effects of maternal cigarette smoking during pregnancy: A research note on the mediating impact of neuropsychological deficit. *Journal of Research in Crime and Delinquency* 43(4):412–26.

McGloin, J. M., C. J. Sullivan, A. R. Piquero, and T. C. Pratt. 2007. Local life circumstances and offending specialization/versatility: Comparing opportunity and propensity models. *Journal of Research in Crime and Delinquency* 44:321–46.

McGloin, J. M., and C. S. Widom. 2001. Resilience among abused and neglected children grown up. *Development and Psychopathology* 13:1021–38.

McKelvey, B. 1977. *American prisons.* Montclair, NJ: Patterson Smith.

Mears, D. P. 2003. A critique of waiver research: Critical next steps in assessing the impacts of laws for transferring juveniles to the criminal justice system. *Youth Violence and Juvenile Justice* 1:156–72.

———. 2007. Towards rational and evidence-based crime policy. *Journal of Criminal Justice* 35:667–82.

Mears, D. P., C. Hay, M. Gertz, and C. Mancini. 2007. Public opinion and the foundation of the juvenile court. *Criminology* 45:223–58.

Megargee, E. 1976. The association of population density, reduced space, and uncomfortable temperatures with misconduct in a prison community. *American Journal of Community Psychology* 5:289–98.

Messner, S. F., and R. Rosenfeld. 2001. *Crime and the American Dream.* 3rd ed. Belmont, CA: Wadsworth.

Methvin, E. H. 2006. Mugged by reality. In *Taking sides: Clashing views in crime and criminology,* ed. T. Hickey, 7th ed., 341–50. Dubuque, IA: McGraw-Hill.

Miller, J. 1991. *Last one over the wall: The Massachusetts experiment in closing reform schools.* Columbus: Ohio State University Press.

———. 1996. *Search and destroy: African American males in the criminal justice system.* New York: Cambridge University Press.

Miller, S. 2003. Summer of the shark? *Spiked* July 24.

Mitford, J. 1971. *Kind and usual punishment: The prison business.* New York: Vintage.

Moffitt, T. E. 1993. Adolescence-limited and life-course persistent antisocial behavior: A developmental taxonomy. *Psychological Review* 100:674–701.

Moon, M. M., J. L. Sundt, J. P. Wright, and F. T. Cullen. 2000. Is child saving dead? Public support for juvenile rehabilitation. *Crime & Delinquency* 46:38–60.

Mooney, C. 2006. *The Republican war on science.* New ed. New York: Basic Books.

Moore, D. W. 1994. Public wants crime bill. *The Gallup Poll Monthly* 347(August):11.

———. 1995. Americans firmly support death penalty. *The Gallup Poll Monthly* 357(June):23–25.

Morash, M., R. N. Haarr, and L. Rucker. 1994. A comparison of programming for women and men in U.S. prisons in the 1980s. *Crime & Delinquency* 40:197–221.

Morris, N., and M. Tonry. 1990. *Between prison and probation: Intermediate punishments in a rational sentencing system.* New York: Oxford University Press.

Mosher, C. J., and S. Akins. 2007. *Drugs and drug policy: The control of consciousness alteration.* Thousand Oaks, CA: Sage Publications.

Muircheartaigh, C. 1997. Measurement error in surveys: A historical perspective. In *Survey measurement and process quality,* ed. L. Lyberg et al. New York: Wiley.

Mullen, J. 1985. Corrections and the private sector. *The Prison Journal* 65:1–13.

Murray, C. 1984. *Losing ground: American social policy, 1950–1980.* New York: Basic Books.

Nacci, P. L., and T. R. Kane. 1983. The incidence of sex and sexual aggression in federal prisons. *Federal Probation* 47:31–6.

Nagel, W. 1977. On behalf of a moratorium on prison construction. *Crime & Delinquency* 23:152–74.

Nagin, D. 1978. Crime rates, sanction levels, and constraints on prison population. *Law and Society Review* 12:341–66.

———. 1998a. Criminal deterrence research at the outset of the twenty-first century. In vol. 23 of *Crime and justice: A review of research,* ed. M. Tonry and N. Morris. Chicago: University of Chicago Press.

———. 1998b. Deterrence and incapacitation. In *The handbook of crime and punishment,* ed. M. Tonry. New York: Oxford University Press.

Nagin, D., and K. C. Land. 1993. Age, criminal careers, and population heterogeneity: Specification and estimation of a non-parametric, mixed Poisson model. *Criminology* 31:327–62.

Nagin, D. S., and G. Pogarsky. 2003. An experimental investigation of deterrence: Cheating, self-serving bias, and impulsivity. *Criminology* 41:167–93.

Nardulli, P., J. Eisenstein, and R. Flemming. 1988. *The tenor of justice.* Chicago: University of Chicago Press.

National Institute on Money in State Politics. 2002. *Prison companies give $1.1 million to campaigns in southern states.* Available at http://www.followthemoney.org/press/ReportView.phtml?r=90.

Neuman, W. R. 1986. *The paradox of mass politics: Knowledge and opinion in the American electorate.* Cambridge, MA: Harvard University Press.

Newman, G. 1985. *The punishment response.* Albany, NY: Harrow and Heston.

Ogle, R. S. 1999. Prison privatization: An environmental catch-22. *Justice Quarterly* 16:579–600.

Orfield, G., and S. Eaton. 1996. *Dismantling desegregation: The quiet reversal of Brown v. Board of Education.* New York: The New Press.

Packer, H. L. 1968. *The limits of the criminal sanction.* Stanford, CA: Stanford University Press.

Palmer, T. 1974. The Youth Authority's community treatment project. *Federal Probation* 38(1):3–14.

———. 1975. Martinson revisited. *Journal of Research in Crime and Delinquency* 12:133–52.

———. 1992. *The re-emergence of correctional intervention.* Thousand Oaks, CA: Sage Publications.

Palmer, T., and R. Lewis. 1980. A differentiated approach to juvenile diversion. *Journal of Research in Crime and Delinquency* 17:209–29.

Paternoster, R. 1987. The deterrent effect of the perceived certainty and severity of punishment: A review of the evidence and issues. *Justice Quarterly* 4:173–217.

Perrone, D., and T. C. Pratt. 2003. Comparing the quality of confinement and cost effectiveness of public versus private prisons: What we know, why we don't know more, and where to go from here. *The Prison Journal* 83:301–22.

Perrone, D., C. Sullivan, S. Margaryan, and T. C. Pratt. 2004. Parental efficacy, self-control, and delinquent behavior: A test of a general theory of crime on a nationally-representative sample. *International Journal of Offender Therapy and Comparative Criminology* 48:298–312.

Petersilia, J. 1980. Criminal career research: A review of recent evidence. In vol. 2 of *Crime and justice: A review of research,* ed. N. Morris and M. Tonry. Chicago: University of Chicago Press.

———. 1998. A crime control rationale for reinvesting in community corrections. In *Community corrections: Probation, parole, and intermediate sanctions,* ed. J. Petersilia, 20–8. New York: Oxford University Press.

———. 2003. *When prisoners come home: Parole and prisoner reentry.* New York: Oxford University Press.

Petersilia, J., and S. Turner. 1990. *Intensive supervision for high-risk probationers: Findings from three California experiments.* Santa Monica, CA: RAND.

———. 1993. Intensive probation and parole. In vol. 17 of *Crime and justice: A review of research,* ed. M. Tonry, 281–335. Chicago: University of Chicago Press.

Peterson, R. D., and W. C. Bailey. 1991. Felony murder and capital punishment: An examination of the deterrence question. *Criminology* 29:367–95.

Pew Charitable Trusts. 2008. *One in 100: Behind bars in America 2008*. Public Safety Performance Project. Washington, DC: Author. Available online at http://www.pewtrusts.org/uploadedFiles/wwwpewtrustsorg/Reports/sentencing_and_corrections/one_in_100.pdf.

Piquero, A. R., R. Brame, and D. Lynam. 2004. Studying criminal career length through early adulthood among serious offenders. *Crime & Delinquency* 50:412–35.

Piquero, A. R., D. P. Farrington, and A. Blumstein. 2003. The criminal career paradigm. In vol. 30 of *Crime and justice: A review of research,* ed. M. Tonry. Chicago: University of Chicago Press.

Piquero, A., and S. Tibbetts. 1996. Specifying the direct and indirect effects of low self-control and situational factors in offenders' decision making: Toward a more complete model of rational offending. *Justice Quarterly* 13:481–510.

Pizarro, J. M., V. M. K. Stenius, and T. C. Pratt. 2006. Supermax prisons: Myths, realities, and the politics of punishment in American society. *Criminal Justice Policy Review* 17:6–21.

Platt, A. M. 1969. *The child savers: The invention of delinquency.* Chicago: University of Chicago Press.

Pratt, T. C. 1998. Race and sentencing: A meta-analysis of conflicting empirical research results. *Journal of Criminal Justice* 26:513–23.

———. 2002. Meta-analysis and its discontents: Treatment destruction techniques revisited. *Journal of Offender Rehabilitation* 35:23–40.

———. 2008. Rational choice theory, crime control policy, and criminological relevance. *Criminology and Public Policy* 7(1):43–52.

Pratt, T. C., and F. T. Cullen. 2000. The empirical status of Gottfredson and Hirschi's general theory of crime: A meta-analysis. *Criminology* 38:931–64.

———. 2005. Macro-level predictors and theories of crime: A meta-analysis. In *Crime and justice: An annual review of research,* ed. M. Tonry. Chicago: University of Chicago Press.

Pratt, T. C., F. T. Cullen, K. R. Blevins, L. E. Daigle, and T. D. Madensen. 2006. The empirical status of deterrence theory: A meta-analysis. In *Taking stock: The empirical status of criminological theory (vol. 15 of Advances in criminological theory),* ed. F. T. Cullen, J. P. Wright, and K. R. Blevins. New Brunswick, NJ: Transaction.

Pratt, T. C., F. T. Cullen, K. R. Blevins, L. Daigle, and J. D. Unnever. 2002. The relationship of attention deficit hyperactivity disorder to crime and delinquency: A meta-analysis. *International Journal of Police Science and Management* 4:344–60.

Pratt, T. C., and T. W. Godsey. 2002. Social support and homicide: A cross-national test of an emerging criminological theory. *Journal of Criminal Justice* 30:589–601.

———. 2003. Social support, inequality, and homicide: A cross-national test of an integrated theoretical model. *Criminology* 41:101–33.

Pratt, T. C., and C. T. Lowenkamp. 2002. Conflict theory, economic conditions, and homicide: A time series analysis. *Homicide Studies* 6:61–83.

Pratt, T. C., and J. Maahs. 1999. Are private prisons more cost-effective than public prisons? A meta-analysis of evaluation research studies. *Crime & Delinquency* 45:358–71.

Pratt, T. C., J. R. Maahs, and S. D. Stehr. 1998. The symbolic ownership of the corrections "problem": A framework for understanding the development of corrections policy in the United States. *The Prison Journal* 78:451–64.

Pratt, T. C., J. M. McGloin, and N. E. Fearn. 2006. Maternal cigarette smoking during pregnancy and criminal/deviant behavior: A meta-analysis. *International Journal of Offender Therapy and Comparative Criminology* 50:672–90.

Pratt, T. C., M. G. Turner, and A. R. Piquero. 2004. Parental socialization and community context: A longitudinal analysis of the structural sources of low self-control. *Journal of Research in Crime and Delinquency* 41:219–43.

Pratt, T. C., and M. R. Winston. 1999. The search for the frugal grail: An empirical assessment of the cost-effectiveness of public versus private correctional facilities. *Criminal Justice Policy Review* 10:447–71.

Putnam, R. D. 2000. *Bowling alone: The collapse and revival of American community.* New York: Simon & Schuster.

Reichel, P. L., and A. K. Gauthier. 1990. Boot camp corrections: A public reaction. In *Issues in justice: Explaining policy issues in the criminal justice system,* ed. R. Muraskin. Bristol, IN: Wyndham Hall Press.

Reiman, J. 2004. *The rich get richer and the poor get prison.* 7th ed. Boston: Pearson.

Reisig, M. D. 2002. Administrative control and inmate homicide. *Homicide Studies* 6:84–103.

Reisig, M. D., W. D. Bales, C. Hay, and X. Wang. 2007. The effect of racial inequality on black male recidivism. *Justice Quarterly* 24:408–34.

Reisig, M. D., and T. C. Pratt. 2000. The ethics of correctional privatization: A critical examination of the delegation of coercive authority. *The Prison Journal* 80:210–22.

Renzema, M. 1992. Home confinement programs: Development, implementation, and impact. In *Smart sentencing: The emergence of intermediate sanctions,* ed. J. M. Byrne, A. J. Lurigio, and J. Petersilia, 41–53. Newbury Park, CA: Sage Publications.

Reynolds, M. O. 1996. *Crime and punishment in Texas: An update.* Dallas, TX: National Center for Policy Analysis.

Richardson, W. 2000. Criminal behavior fueled by attention deficit hyperactivity disorder and addiction. In *The Science, treatment, and prevention of antisocial behaviors: Application to the criminal justice system,* ed. D. H. Fishbein, 18-1 to 18-15. Kingston, NJ: Civic Research Institute.

Roberts, J. V. 1992. Public opinion, crime, and criminal justice. In vol. 16 of *Crime and justice: A review of research,* ed. M. Tonry. Chicago: University of Chicago Press.

Roberts, J. V., and L. J. Stalans. 1997. *Public opinion, crime, and criminal justice.* Boulder, CO: Westview Press.

Rose, D. A., and T. R. Clear. 1998. Incarceration, social capital, and crime: Implications for social disorganization theory. *Criminology* 36:441–79.

Rossi, P. H., and R. A. Berk. 1997. *Just punishments: Federal guidelines and public views compared.* New York: de Gruyter.

Rossi, P. H., R. A. Berk, and A. Campbell. 1997. Just punishments: Guideline sentences and normative consensus. *Journal of Quantitative Criminology* 13:267–90.

Rothman, D. 1971. *The discovery of the asylum: Social order and disorder in the new republic.* Boston: Little, Brown.

———. 1980. *Conscience and convenience: The asylum and its alternatives in progressive America.* Boston: Little, Brown.

Rubin, A., E. M. Perse, and D. S. Taylor. 1988. A methodological examination of cultivation. *Communication Research* 15:107–34.

Sabol, W. J., and J. P. Lynch. 2003. Assessing the longer-run consequences of incarceration: Effects on families and employment. In *Crime control and social justice: The delicate balance,* ed. D. Hawkins, S. L. Myers, and R. Stone. Westport, CT: Greenwood Press.

Sampson, R. J. 1987. Urban black violence: The effect of male joblessness and family disruption. *American Journal of Sociology* 93:348–82.

———. 2006. Collective efficacy theory: Lessons learned and directions for future inquiry. In *Taking stock: The status of criminological theory (vol. 15 of Advances in criminological theory),* ed. F. T. Cullen, J. P. Wright, and K. R. Blevins. New Brunswick, NJ: Transaction.

Sampson, R. J., and J. Cohen. 1988. Deterrent effects of the police on crime: A replication and theoretical extension. *Law and Society Review* 22:163–89.

Sampson, R. J., and W. B. Groves. 1989. Community structure and crime: Testing social-disorganization theory. *American Journal of Sociology* 94:774–802.

Sampson, R. J., and J. H. Laub. 1993. *Crime in the making: Pathways and turning points through life.* Cambridge, MA: Harvard University Press.

Sampson, R. J., and S. W. Raudenbush. 1999. Systematic social observation of public spaces: A new look at disorder in urban neighborhoods. *American Journal of Sociology* 105:603–51.

Sampson, R. J., S. W. Raudenbush, and F. Earls. 1997. Neighborhoods and violent crime: A multilevel study of collective efficacy. *Science* 227:916–24.

Sampson, R. J., and W. J. Wilson. 1995. Toward a theory of race, crime, and urban inequality. In *Crime and inequality,* ed. J. Hagan and R. D. Peterson. Stanford, CA: Stanford University Press.

Sandys, M., and E. F. McGarrell. 1995. Attitudes toward capital punishment: Preference for the death penalty or mere acceptance? *Journal of Research in Crime and Delinquency* 32:191–213.

Scacco, A. M. 1984. What all this means—can anything be done to affect change? In *Male rape: A casebook of sexual aggression,* ed. A. M. Scacco, 298–315. New York: AMS Press.

Schor, J. B. 1992. *The overworked American.* New York: Basic Books.

Schuman, H., and S. Presser. 1981. *Questions and answers in attitude surveys: Experiment on question form, wording, and context.* New York: Academic Press.

Schur, E. 1971. *Labeling deviant behavior.* New York: Harper & Row.

Schwartz, M. D., and D. M. Nurge. 2004. Capitalist punishment: Ethics and private prisons. *Critical Criminology* 12:133–56.

Scull, A. 1977. *Decarceration: Community treatment and the deviant—a radical view.* Englewood Cliffs, NJ: Prentice Hall.

Semple, J. 1993. *Bentham's prison: A study of the panopticon penitentiary.* Oxford, UK: Clarendon Press.

Senese, J. D. 1992. Intensive supervision probation and public opinion: Perceptions of community correctional policy and practice. *American Journal of Criminal Justice* 16:33–56.

Shaffer, D. K. 2006. Reconsidering drug court effectiveness: A meta-analytic review. Unpublished doctoral dissertation, University of Cincinnati, Ohio.

Shannon, L. W. 1991. *Changing patterns of delinquency and crime: A longitudinal study in Racine.* Boulder, CO: Westview Press.

Shaw, C., and H. McKay. 1942. *Juvenile delinquency in urban areas.* Chicago: University of Chicago Press.

Sheehy, G. 2000. The accidental candidate. *Vanity Fair,* October (retrieved online, May, 2008).

Sherman, L. W., P. R. Gartin, and M. E. Buerger. 1989. Hot spots of predatory crime: Routine activities and the criminology of place. *Criminology* 27:27–56.

Sherman, L. W., D. Gottredson, D. L. MacKenzie, J. Eck, P. Reuter, and S. Bushway. 1997. *Preventing crime: What works, what doesn't, what's promising.* Washington, DC: National Institute of Justice.

Shichor, D. 1992. Myths and realities in prison siting. *Crime & Delinquency* 38:70–87.

———. 1995. *Punishment for profit: Private prisons/public concerns.* Thousand Oaks, CA: Sage Publications.

Skogan, W. 1990. *Disorder and decline: Crime and the spiral of decay in American neighborhoods.* New York: Free Press.

Smith, N. E., and M. E. Batiuk. 1989. Sexual victimization and inmate social interaction. *The Prison Journal* 2:29–38.

Smith, T. W. 1998. Trendlets: B. Crime and punishment: An update. *GSS News* 12(August):5.

Snyder, H. N., and M. Sickmund. 2006. *Juvenile offenders and victims: 2006 national report.* Washington, DC: Office of Juvenile Justice and Delinquency Prevention.

Sparks, R. 1992. *Television and the drama of crime: Moral tales and the place of crime in public life.* Buckingham, UK: Open University Press.

Spelman, W. 1994. *Criminal incapacitation.* New York: Plenum.

———. 2000. The limited importance of prison expansion. In *The crime drop in America,* ed. A. Blumstein and J. Wallman, 97–129. Cambridge, UK: Cambridge University Press.

Spohn, C. 2007. The deterrent effect of imprisonment and offenders' stakes in conformity. *Criminal Justice Policy Review* 18:31–50.

Stanley, L. L. 1940. *Men at their worst.* New York: D. Appleton/Century Company.

Staples, W. 1990. *Castles of our conscience.* New Brunswick, NJ: Rutgers University Press.

Steelman, S., and K. Harms. 1986. Construction management firms: Saving time and money. *Corrections Today* 48:64–6.

Stolz, B. A. 2002. *Criminal justice policy making: Federal roles and processes.* Westport, CT: Praeger.

Struckman-Johnson, C., D. Struckman-Johnson, L. Rucker, K. Bumby, and S. Donaldson. 1996. Sexual coercion reported by men and women in prison. *Journal of Sex Research* 33:67–76.

Sullivan, C. J., J. M. McGloin, T. C. Pratt, and A. R. Piquero. 2006. Rethinking the "norm" of offender generality: Investigating specialization in the short term. *Criminology* 44:199–233.

Sullivan, C. J., B. M. Veysey, and L. Dorangrichia. 2003. Violent offending in high-risk youth: Examining problem history as a problem behavior. *Journal of Offender Rehabilitation* 38:17–39.

Sullivan, M. L. 1989. *Getting paid: Youth, crime, and work in the inner city*. Ithaca, NY: Cornell University Press.

Sundt, J. L., F. T. Cullen, B. K. Applegate, and M. G. Turner. 1998. The tenacity of the rehabilitative ideal revisited: Have attitudes toward rehabilitation changed? *Criminal Justice and Behavior* 25:426–42.

Sykes, G. 1958. *The society of captives.* Princeton, NJ: Princeton University Press.

Tamaki, J. 2000. Prison is town's savior, but at a price. *Los Angeles Times.* March 7, A1.

Taxman, F. S., and J. A. Bouffard. 2005. Treatment as part of drug court: The implications on graduation rates. *Journal of Offender Rehabilitation* 42:23–50.

Taylor, R. B., and M. Hale. 1986. Testing alternative models of fear of crime. *Journal of Criminal Law and Criminology* 77:151–89.

Thomson, D. R., and A. J. Ragona. 1987. Popular moderation versus governmental authoritarianism: An interactionist view of public sentiments toward criminal sanctions. *Crime & Delinquency* 33:332–37.

Toby, J. 1964. Is punishment necessary? *Journal of Criminal Law, Criminology, and Police Science* 55:332–37.

Tonry, M. 1995. *Malign neglect: Race, crime, and punishment in America.* New York: Oxford University Press.

———. 1998. Intermediate sanctions in sentencing guidelines. In vol. 23 of *Crime and justice: A Review of research,* ed. M. Tonry. Chicago: University of Chicago Press.

Travis, J., and S. Lawrence. 2002. *Beyond the prison gates: The state of parole in America*. Washington, DC: The Urban Institute.

Triplett, R. 1996. The growing threat: Gangs and juvenile offenders. In *Americans view crime and justice: A national public opinion survey,* ed. T. J. Flanagan and D. R. Longmire. Thousand Oaks, CA: Sage Publications.

Turner, M. G., F. T. Cullen, J. L. Sundt, and B. K. Applegate. 1997. Public tolerance for community-based sanctions. *Prison Journal* 77:6–26.

Turner, M. G., A. R. Piquero, and T. C. Pratt. 2005. The school context as a source of self-control. *Journal of Criminal Justice* 33:327–39.

Unnever, J. D., and F. T. Cullen. 2005. Executing the innocent and support for capital punishment: Implications for public policy. *Criminology and Public Policy* 4:3–38.

Unnever, J. D., F. T. Cullen, and T. C. Pratt. 2003. Parental management, ADHD, and delinquent involvement: Reassessing Gottfredson and Hirschi's general theory. *Justice Quarterly* 20:471–500.

Unnever, J. D., J. V. Roberts, and F. T. Cullen. 2005. Not everyone strongly supports the death penalty: Assessing weakly-held attitudes about capital punishment. *American Journal of Criminal Justice* 20:187–216.

U.S. Census Bureau. 2000. *United States Census 2000.* Available online at http://www.census.gov/main/www/cen2000.html.

Useem, B., and M. D. Reisig. 1999. Collective action in prisons: Protests, disturbances, and riots. *Criminology* 37:735–60.

Visher, C. A. 1986. The RAND inmate survey: A reanalysis. In *Criminal careers and "career criminals,"* ed. A. Blumstein, J. Cohen, J. A. Roth, and C. A. Visher. Washington, DC: National Academy Press.

———. 1987. Incapacitation and crime control: Does a "lock 'em up" strategy reduce crime? *Justice Quarterly* 4:513–43.

Visher, C. A., and J. Travis. 2003. Transitions from prison to community: Understanding individual pathways. *Annual Review of Sociology* 29:89–113.

von Hirsch, A. 1984. The ethics of selective incapacitation: Observations on the contemporary debate. *Crime & Delinquency* 30:175–94.

———. 1985. *Past or future crimes: Deservedness and dangerousness in the sentencing of criminals.* New Brunswick, NJ: Rutgers University Press.

Walker, L., and B. Wilson. 2002. *Black Eden.* East Lansing: Michigan State University Press.

Walker, S. 2001. *Sense and nonsense about crime and drugs.* 5th ed. Belmont, CA: Wadsworth/Thomson.

Ward, D. A., and C. R. Tittle. 1994. IQ and delinquency: A test of two competing explanations. *Journal of Quantitative Criminology* 10:189–212.

Warr, M. 1980. The accuracy of public beliefs about crime. *Social Forces* 59:470.

———. 1982. The accuracy of public beliefs about crime: Further evidence. *Criminology* 20:185–204.

———. 1994. Public perceptions and reactions to violent offending and victimization. In vol. 4 of *Understanding and preventing violence: Consequences and control,* ed. A. J. Reiss and J. A. Roth. Washington, DC: National Academy Press.

———. 1995. Public perceptions of crime and punishment. In *Criminology: A contemporary handbook,* ed. J. F. Sheley, 2nd ed. Belmont, CA: Wadsworth.

Warr, M., and M. Stafford. 1984. Public goals of punishment and support for the death penalty. *Journal of Research in Crime and Delinquency* 21:95–111.

Watts, R. K., and D. Glaser. 1992. Electronic monitoring of drug offenders in California. In *Smart sentencing: The emergence of intermediate sanctions,* ed. J. M. Byrne, A. J. Lurigio, and J. Petersilia, 68–84. Newbury Park, CA: Sage Publications.

Weimer, D. L., and A. R. Vining. 1992. *Policy analysis: Concepts and practice.* 2nd ed. Englewood Cliffs, NJ: Prentice Hall.

Weisburd, D., T. Einat, and M. Kowalski. 2008. The miracle of the cells: An experimental study of interventions to increase payment of court-ordered financial obligations. *Criminology and Public Policy* 7(1):9–36.

Wells-Parker, E., and R. Bangert-Drowns. 1991. Meta-analysis of research on DUI remedial interventions. *Alcohol, Drugs and Driving* 6:147–60.

Western, B. 2002. The impact of incarceration on wage mobility and inequality. *American Sociological Review* 67:526–46.

Western, B., J. R. Kling, and D. F. Weiman. 2001. The labor market consequences of incarceration. *Crime & Delinquency* 47:410–27.

Wilbanks, W. 1987. *The myth of a racist criminal justice system.* Monterey, CA: Brooks/Cole.

Wildavsky, A. 1979. *Speaking truth to power: The art and craft of policy analysis.* Boston: Little, Brown.

Wilson, J.Q. 1975. *Thinking about crime.* New York: Vintage.

———. 1996. What to do about crime. In *What to do about . . . ,* ed. N. Kozodoy. New York: Harper Collins.

———. 1997. *Moral judgment.* New York: Basic Books.

Wilson, J. Q., and B. Boland. 1978. The effect of police on crime. *Law and Society Review* 12:367–90.

Wilson, J. Q., and R. J. Herrnstein. 1985. *Crime and human nature: The definitive study of the causes of crime.* New York: Simon & Schuster.

Wilson, J. Q., and G. Kelling. 1982. Broken windows. *Atlantic Monthly.* March:29–38.

Wilson, W. J. 1987. *The truly disadvantaged.* Chicago: University of Chicago Press.

———. 1996. *When work disappears.* New York: Vintage Books.

Winerip, M. (1999). Bedlam on the streets: Increasingly the mentally ill have no place to go. *New York Times Magazine.* May 23:42–70.

Winston, M. R., and T. C. Pratt. 1999. The search for the frugal grail: An empirical assessment of the cost-effectiveness of public versus private correctional facilities. *Criminal Justice Policy Review* 10:447–71.

Wolfgang, M. E., R. M. Figlio, and T. Sellin. 1972. *Delinquency in a birth cohort.* Chicago: University of Chicago Press.

Wooldredge, J. 1994. Inmate crime and victimization in a southwestern correctional facility. *Journal of Criminal Justice* 22:367–81.

———. 1998. Inmate lifestyle and opportunities for victimization. *Journal of Research in Crime and Delinquency* 35:480–502.

Wooldredge, J., T. Griffin, and T. C. Pratt. 2001. Considering hierarchical models for research on inmate behavior: Predicting misconduct with multilevel data. *Justice Quarterly* 18:203–31.

World Health Organization. 2000. *World Health Report 2000.* Geneva: Author.

Worrall, J. L. 2001. Addicted to the drug war: The role of civil asset forfeiture as a budgetary necessity in contemporary law enforcement. *Journal of Criminal Justice* 29:171–87.

Wright, J. D., and P. H. Rossi. 1986. *Armed and considered dangerous: A survey of felons and their firearms.* New York: Aldine de Gruyter.

Wright, J. P., and K. M. Beaver. 2005. Do parents matter in creating self-control in their children? A genetically informed test of Gottfredson and Hirschi's theory of low self-control. *Criminology* 43:1169–203.

Yoshikawa, H. 1994. Prevention as cumulative protection: Effects of early family support and education on chronic delinquency and its risks. *Psychological Bulletin* 115:28–54.

Young, J. 1987. The tasks facing a realist criminology. *Contemporary Crises* 11:337–56.

Young, W., and M. Brown. 1993. Cross-national comparisons of imprisonment. In vol. 17 of *Crime and justice: An annual review of research,* ed. M. Tonry. Chicago: University of Chicago Press.

Zedlewski, E. W. 1987. *Making confinement decisions.* Washington, DC: Government Printing Office.

Zimring, F. E., and G. Hawkins. 1988. The new mathematics of imprisonment. *Crime & Delinquency* 34:425–36.

———. 1995. *Incapacitation: Penal confinement and the restraint of crime.* New York: Oxford University Press.

———. 1997. *Crime is not the problem: Lethal violence in America.* New York: Oxford University Press.

Court Cases Cited

Brooks v. Florida, 389 U.S. 413 (1967).

Brown v. Board of Education of Topeka, Kansas, 347 U.S. 483 (1954).

Furman v. Georgia, 408 U.S. 238 (1972).

Holt v. Sarver, 442 F.2d 308 (8th Cir. 1971).

Index

Note: In page references, f indicates figures and t indicates tables.

About the Author

Travis C. Pratt received his degrees from Washington State University (BA, Political Science; MA, Criminal Justice) and the University of Cincinnati (PhD, Criminal Justice). He has been on the faculty of the School of Criminal Justice at Rutgers University–Newark, and was the Director of the Program in Criminal Justice at Washington State University before joining the School of Criminology and Criminal Justice at Arizona State University, where he is currently an Associate Professor.

His research and publications focus primarily on structural and integrated theories of crime and delinquency (including macro-level, multi-level, and individual-level approaches to the study of criminal/deviant behavior) and correctional policy (both institutional and community corrections). He has published over 40 articles that have appeared in the leading peer-reviewed journals in the field, including *Crime & Delinquency, Crime and Justice: A Review of Research, Criminology, Journal of Research in Crime and Delinquency,* and *Justice Quarterly.* He received the 2006 Ruth Shonle Cavan Outstanding Young Scholar Award from the American Society of Criminology for his research and scholarship.

About the Author